D0380971

Allergy Free Cooking

A Family Friendly Cookbook

By Victoria Mazur

Copyright @ 2013 by Victoria Mazur

All Rights Reserved

This book is not intended to provide or replace the medical expertise of a trusted physician. If you have a serious food allergy, you should consult with your doctor before making any decisions that affect your health. While the recipes in this book do not require the use of any ingredients containing gluten, dairy, eggs, soy, shellfish, or nuts, remember to check the labels of all products you purchase to ensure they do not contain any such allergens. While every effort was made to check the allergy-free status of the foods listed, manufacturers are often changing their formulas. It is the reader's responsibility to double check the allergy-free status of your foods. If you are unsure, contact the manufacturer directly.

DEDICATION

To Ryan, my most amazing husband.

To my sons Steven, David and Adam, you make me proud every day.

To my daughter Sarah, my angel face mini-me.

To my daughter-in-law Nicole, I'm so lucky to have you in my life.

.

INTRODUCTION

I decided to write this cookbook after I married into a family with multiple food allergies. I have always been the primary cook in the house, so if someone had food issues, I had to find a solution. After buying many "allergy free" and "gluten free" cookbooks that use expensive and hard to find substitutions in their recipes, I knew that wasn't the answer for me and my family. Have you ever tried to find xanthan gum at your local grocery store? Good luck! And let's be honest, a lot of the substitution recipes are simply not very tasty, especially if you're also cooking for family and friends without food allergies.

I decided to create a book of recipes that do not rely on specialty store items, that your family and friends can enjoy together, whether you have a food allergy or not. The recipes in this book don't require any fancy ingredients or a lot of cooking experience to prepare. Rather than reinvent entire recipes from scratch, I have simply brought together recipes that my family has enjoyed for years, that don't use the most common food allergens: gluten, dairy, eggs, soy, shellfish, and nuts.

I am not a chef, I just cook dinner six nights a week and really like food. The recipes are grouped into complete dinners that can be switched around depending on your personal preference. Most of these recipes serve four, but can be modified to fit your needs.

One final note for those of you with a serious food allergy. While each of these recipes is free of any gluten, dairy, eggs, soy, shellfish, or nuts, please remember to check the labels before you buy your groceries. For instance, I have a couple recipes with Worcestershire sauce in them, and several brands include gluten and soy. *Lea and Perrins* is the only Worcestershire sauce I know that is both gluten and soy free.

Contents

Soups

I always have basic stocks on hand for everyday cooking. If you are able to find a store-bought stock that is allergy free and tastes good, by all means use that shortcut. I am a bit of a "stock snob," so I usually make my own. If you do decide to use store bought stocks, I have found that mixing beef and chicken stock together provides a more homemade taste.

Vegetable Broth

This is a very flavorful broth that I use in all our vegetarian meals. I also use this when I am making vegetable dishes or more delicate fish dishes. The roasted vegetables really add to the flavor. However, they will darken the broth.

Vegetable broth

3 onions, quartered
6 celery stalks, halved
1 lb. mushrooms
3 peppers, quartered
5 carrots, halved
2 T vegetable oil
1 gal water
2 bay leaves
8 sprigs of fresh thyme
1 T salt
½ t pepper

Preheat the oven to 425°. Divide the onions, celery, mushrooms, peppers and carrots onto two cookie sheets. Add 1 tablespoon of vegetable oil to each cookie sheet and roast in the oven for 45 minutes until browned, stirring every ten minutes. Scrape the vegetables into a large stock pot and add water, salt, pepper, bay leaves and thyme. Bring the water to a boil, cover and reduce to a simmer for 1 hour. Strain well. Cool and store in the freezer.

Chicken Stock

I usually save the chicken parts that we don't care for, like the wings and backs, in the freezer until I am ready to make stock. If I am running short on freezer space, before I store in the freezer I will boil the stock over medium heat until the stock is reduced by half. I can then freeze the stock in ice cube trays for easier storage. When I am ready to use the stock, I simply add equal parts stock and water to whatever dish I am making.

Chicken stock

2 whole chickens or 4 lbs of pieces
3 onions, quartered
5 celery stalks, halved
5 carrots, halved
1 gal water
2 bay leaves
10 sprigs of fresh thyme
1 T salt
1 t pepper

In a large stock pot over medium-high heat, combine chicken, onions, celery, carrots and water. Bring the water to a boil then reduce heat to a simmer. For the first ½ hour remove scum from the top of the pot every 15 minutes. Add the bay leaves, thyme, salt and pepper to the pot. Simmer partly covered for 4 hours. Strain well. Cool to room temperature then refrigerate overnight. The fat will congeal on the top of the stock. Lift the fat off the stock and store the chicken stock in the freezer.

Beef Stock

Beef bones can be expensive at the grocery store, so I will save bones from steaks and roasts whenever I can. They freeze wonderfully and then are ready for the stock pot. I don't like to use very fatty meat for this recipe because it leaves the finished stock a little greasy.

Beef stock

2 lbs beef bones
1 lb beef, cubed
3 onions, quartered
5 celery stalks, halved
½ lb mushrooms
5 carrots, halved
2 T tomato paste
1 T vegetable oil
1 gal water
2 bay leaves
8 springs of fresh thyme
1 T salt
1 t pepper

Preheat the oven to 425°. Combine the onions, celery, mushrooms and carrots with vegetable oil. Place beef bones and vegetables on a cookie sheet and roast in the oven for 45 minutes until browned. Scrape bones and vegetables into a stock pot and add water. Add the cubed beef. Bring to a boil then reduce heat to a simmer. For the first ½ hour remove scum from the top of the pot every 15 minutes. Add the tomato paste, salt, pepper, bay leaves, and thyme. Simmer partly covered for 5 hours. Strain well. Cool to room temperature then refrigerate overnight. The fat will congeal on the top of the stock. Lift the fat off the stock and store the beef stock in the freezer.

Minestrone Soup

This was my grandma's recipe. It's a very hardy soup that is great for lunch or dinner. If desired, this soup can be made early in the day and reheated before serving. Reserve the fresh basil and add just before reheating. I freeze any leftover soup and simply reheat when needed.

Minestrone soup
Timing to table: 1 ½ hours
Serves 10

2 medium carrots, peeled and sliced
1 large onion, diced
2 celery stalks, diced
1 small head cabbage, coarsely shredded
6 oz spinach
8 oz kale, de-stemmed and chopped
1 (28-oz) can whole tomatoes with juice
8 oz frozen green beans
2 medium red potatoes, peeled and cubed
2 (15-oz) cans cannellini beans, drained
1 medium zucchini, diced
2 T vegetable oil
8 c vegetable broth
½ c fresh basil
1 ½ t dried basil
2 t salt
½ t pepper

In large stock pot, heat vegetable oil over medium-high heat. Add carrots, onions and celery. Cook 4 minutes until they begin to soften, then add cabbage, spinach and kale. When the greens begin to wilt (about 6 minutes), add tomatoes. Using a spoon, slightly break up the tomatoes. Add vegetable broth, salt, pepper and dried basil. Bring to a boil, reduce heat, cover and simmer for 15 minutes. Add green beans and potatoes and simmer for 20 minutes. Add cannellini beans and zucchini and simmer another 20 minutes. Stir in fresh basil before serving.

Lentil Soup

This is a delicious vegetarian soup, and the lentils add protein and body to satisfy meat eaters as well. I like to spice my soup up with a little hot sauce right before serving.

Lentil soup
Timing to table: 1 ½ hours
Serves 6

1 lb dried lentils
4 medium carrots, peeled and sliced
1 large onion, diced
1 T vegetable oil
6 c vegetable broth
2 c water
1 bay leaf
1 t cumin
½ t salt
¼ t pepper

In a stock pot over medium heat, heat vegetable oil. Add carrots and onions and sauté until they begin to soften, about 10 minutes. Add salt, pepper, bay leaf and cumin to the pot. Stir in lentils, vegetable broth and water. Bring the vegetable broth to a boil, reduce heat to low and simmer partially covered for 1 hour or until the lentils are tender. Remove the bay leaf before serving.

Onion Soup

This is my mother's recipe that we had for special occasions growing up. We never used bread or cheese in our soup, so there was no need to alter this recipe to make it allergy-free. The caramelized onions really give this a fabulous flavor, so it is very important to really take the time to caramelize them. If you would like to serve this to vegetarians, replace the beef stock with vegetable broth.

Onion soup
Timing to table: 2 hours
Serves 4

4 c onions, sliced
5 T margarine
5 c beef stock
¼ t pepper

In a large stock pot, melt margarine over medium-low heat. Add the onions and sauté until they are a deep golden brown, about 45 minutes. Add pepper and beef stock. Bring the soup to a boil, reduce the heat to low and simmer for 1 hour.

Chicken and Rice Soup

This is a quick and easy soup that has a ton of flavor. I like using a skinless chicken breast instead of dark meat to ensure the soup doesn't get greasy. I have found that brown rice holds up better in the soup than white rice.

Chicken and rice soup

Timing to table: 2 hours
Serves 8

1 chicken breast, boneless and skinless, diced
4 medium carrots, peeled and sliced
2 celery stalks, sliced
1 medium onion, diced
6 mushrooms, sliced
½ c frozen green beans
1 c frozen peas
½ c brown rice
1 T vegetable oil
4 c water
4 c chicken stock
1 t dried parsley
1 t salt
¼ t pepper

In a stock pot over medium-high heat, heat vegetable oil. Add carrots, celery, onions and mushrooms and sauté 10 minutes, until they begin to brown. Add the chicken to the pot and sauté 5 minutes. Add water, chicken stock, green beans, peas, parsley, salt and pepper. Bring the soup to a boil, reduce to a simmer and cook partially covered for 30 minutes. Add the brown rice and cook an additional hour.

Southwest Chicken Soup

This is a variation on the traditional chicken soup. By changing just a few ingredients, you completely change the taste. This soup can be made spicy or mild depending upon your personal preference. If you like a very spicy soup, add cayenne pepper instead of black pepper.

Southwest chicken soup
Timing to table: 2 hours
Serves 8

1 whole boneless and skinless chicken breast, diced
4 carrots, peeled and sliced
2 celery stalks, sliced
1 medium onion, diced
1 c frozen corn
1 c frozen green beans
½ c brown rice
1 T vegetable oil
4 c water
4 c chicken stock
¼ c fresh cilantro, chopped
1 t cumin
1 t dried oregano
1 t salt
¼ t pepper
Hot sauce to taste

In a stock pot over medium-high heat, heat vegetable oil. Add carrots, celery and onions and sauté 10 minutes, until they begin to brown. Add the chicken to the pot and sauté 5 minutes. Add water, chicken stock, green beans, corn, oregano, cumin, salt and pepper. Bring the soup to a boil, reduce heat to a simmer and cook partially covered for 30 minutes. Add the brown rice and cook an additional hour. Stir in fresh cilantro. Sprinkle hot sauce on to taste.

Split Pea Soup

My son always requests this for his birthday, so I always save the bones from any ham that I cook. I simply freeze the ham bone until I'm ready to make soup. This soup freezes very well but will get thicker. Just add water as necessary when reheating for your desired consistency.

Split pea soup
Timing to table: 2 ½ hours
Serves 6

1 ham bone (or 1 ham steak, diced)
1 lb dried split peas
½ lb carrots, peeled and sliced
1 onion, diced
1 T vegetable oil
8 c water
2 bay leaves
½ t pepper
¼ t salt

In a stock pot, heat vegetable oil over medium heat. Add carrots and onions and sauté about 10 minutes or until they begin to soften. Add the ham bone, split peas, water, bay leaves, salt and pepper. Bring the soup to a boil. Reduce heat to low and simmer partially covered for 2 hours, stirring every half hour, until the soup is thick and creamy. Remove the bay leaves and the bone. Cut off any ham remaining on the bone. Add the ham to the soup.

Beef Vegetable Soup

This is a very rich soup and can easily be made with frozen vegetables to speed up the prep time. I typically use bottom round because it is inexpensive and not very fatty. I have made this with rice instead of potatoes, however would caution against using rice and potatoes together. I found it gives the soup an odd flavor.

Beef vegetable soup
Timing to table: 2 ½ hours
Serves 8

1 lb beef, diced into 1 inch cubes
4 carrots, peeled and sliced
2 celery stalks, sliced
1 small onion, diced
6 mushrooms, sliced
½ c frozen green beans
2 large red potatoes, peeled and diced
1 (14-oz) can whole tomatoes
1 T vegetable oil
4 c water
4 c beef stock
1 t dried thyme
2 t salt
½ t pepper

In a stock pot over medium heat, heat vegetable oil. Add the beef, cooking until it is brown on all sides and most of the fat has been rendered. Remove the meat and reserve on the side. Remove all but 1 tablespoon of fat from the pot. Add carrots, celery, onion and mushrooms to the pot and sauté 5 minutes or until they begin to soften. Return the beef to the pot and add water, beef stock, tomatoes, green beans, potatoes, thyme, salt and pepper. Bring the soup to a boil, reduce heat to a simmer and cook partially covered for 2 hours.

Poultry

Enchilada Chicken Tacos, Mexican Rice, Sautéed Zucchini

This is my way of enjoying enchiladas without needing to use any cheese. I find that by using taco shells instead of tortillas, you still get a lot of great flavor, and you don't miss the cheese and sour cream as much. The enchilada sauce for this recipe has medium spice, and the tomatoes and avocado balance it out nicely.

This Mexican rice is very similar to the rice my children and I get at the taco stand we like. It is very simple yet it complements the enchiladas well. If I have fresh cilantro on hand, I will chop some and add about 1 teaspoon of the cilantro to the top of the rice for a pretty presentation.

I love zucchini and this is the easiest way I know of cooking it. The garlic flavors the oil that the zucchini is sautéed in, and the zucchini ends up with a tender center and a crispy outside. The garlic also sweetens as it browns, making the sliced garlic delicious to eat.

Enchilada chicken tacos
Timing to table: 1 ½ hours
Serves 4

2 chicken breast, skinless
8 taco shells
½ head lettuce, sliced
1 avocado, diced
1 tomato, diced
¼ t salt
¼ t pepper

Enchilada sauce

1 ½ c chicken stock
2 T chili powder
¼ t garlic powder
¼ t cumin
¼ t dried oregano

Preheat the oven to 425°. Sprinkle chicken breasts with salt and pepper. Roast the chicken breasts in the oven for 25 minutes or until they reach an internal temperature of 165°. Remove the chicken and allow it to cool. De-bone then shred the chicken.

In a sauce pan over high heat, combine chicken stock, chili powder, garlic powder, cumin and oregano. Bring the sauce to a boil, cover and reduce heat to low. Simmer 30 minutes. Add the shredded chicken to the sauce and heat through. Fill the taco shells with chicken, lettuce, avocado and tomatoes.

Mexican rice
Timing to table: 30 minutes
Serves 4

1 c rice
2 c chicken stock
1 T tomato paste
½ t cumin
¼ t garlic powder
½ t salt

In a medium sauce pan, bring chicken stock to a boil over high heat. Add the rice, tomato paste, cumin, garlic powder and salt. Reduce the heat to low and simmer covered for 20 minutes or until the rice is tender.

Sautéed zucchini
Timing to table: 20 minutes
Serves 4

2 medium zucchinis, sliced
3 cloves garlic, thinly sliced
2 T olive oil
½ t salt
¼ t pepper

In a large sauté pan, heat olive oil over medium heat. Add garlic and sauté 3 minutes until the garlic is light brown. Add zucchini, salt and pepper. Cook 15 minutes until the zucchini is tender and browned.

Chicken Scampi, Grits, Roasted Green Beans

I love scampi, but the usual shrimp scampi recipes you find are not an option for my family. Using chicken works perfectly. The chicken really takes on the flavor of the lemon and garlic, and the wine and broth make a flavorful light sauce that helps keeps the chicken moist.

I like to serve this over grits, so the grits soak up the scampi sauce. Grits are a cornmeal so they are a perfect gluten-free dish.

The roasted green beans recipe came from my sister-in-law. She mentioned roasting green beans for dinner one day and I immediately tried it. It is now my favorite way to make beans. They are crispy, slightly salty and packed with flavor.

Chicken scampi
Timing to table: 45 minutes
Serves 4

3 chicken breasts, boneless and skinless
1 small onion, finely diced
4 cloves garlic, minced
4 T margarine
2 T olive oil
¼ c chicken stock
¼ c white wine
2 T lemon juice
2 T fresh parsley
½ t salt
Dash of red pepper flakes

In a large sauté pan over medium heat, heat olive oil and margarine. Add the onions to the pan and cook about 10 minutes until they are softened and golden. Slice the chicken about ½ inch thick. Season the chicken with salt, increase the heat to medium high and brown the chicken in the oil and margarine, about 5 minutes. Add the garlic. Add the wine to the pan and allow it to cook down about 5 minutes. Add the chicken stock and red pepper flakes. Cook for 10 minutes until the chicken is no longer pink. Add the lemon juice and the parsley.

Grits
Timing to table: 25 minutes
Serves 4

¾ c grits
3 c chicken stock

In a medium sauce pan bring the chicken stock to a boil and slowly stir in the grits. Reduce the heat to low and simmer for 20 minutes.

Roasted green beans
Timing to table: 25 minutes
Serves 4

1 lb green beans, cleaned
1T olive oil
½ t salt
¼ t pepper

Preheat the oven to 425°. Mix olive oil, green beans, pepper, and salt. Spread beans on a cookie sheet and roast for 25 minutes or until slightly crispy.

Curry Chicken with Broccoli, Jasmine Rice

I use commercial curry powder from the grocery store for this recipe. Just be sure to check the label for anything you may be sensitive to. I use salt in place of the soy sauce that is in more traditional recipes.

I love the fragrance of the jasmine rice, which has a unique floral scent.

Here's a tip on how to make perfect rice; no rice cooker or special skill is needed. I just cook rice like I would pasta. I bring a large pot of water to a boil, add salt and the rice, and cook until the rice is tender. Once it's tender, I just drain the rice and serve.

Chicken curry with broccoli
Timing to table: 25 minutes
Serves 4

2 chicken breasts, skinless and boneless, cut into 1 inch cubes
1 lb broccoli, cut into florets; peel and slice the stems
1 large onions, sliced
4 garlic cloves, sliced
2 T vegetable oil
1 c + 1 T water
1 T cornstarch
1 T curry powder
1 T sugar
1 t salt

In large skillet over medium-high heat, heat the vegetable oil. Add the onions and stir-fry 1 minute. Season the chicken with ½ teaspoon of salt and add the chicken to the skillet. Stir-fry for 2 minutes. Add the broccoli, garlic and curry powder. Stir-fry for another minute. Add sugar, ½ teaspoon of salt and 1 cup of water. Bring mixture to a boil. Reduce the heat to low and cover. Simmer 15 minutes or until chicken is no longer pink and broccoli is tender. In a cup, whisk cornstarch and 1 tablespoon of water together until smooth. Stir cornstarch into the curry chicken. Boil 1 minute or until thickened.

Jasmine rice
Timing to table: 25 minutes
Serves 4

1 c jasmine rice
2 qts water
1 t salt

Bring water to boil in a large sauce pan over high heat. Add the jasmine rice and salt and reduce the heat to medium. Cook uncovered for 20 minutes or until the rice is tender. Drain the rice well.

Chicken Veronique, Tarragon Quinoa, Roasted Asparagus & Prosciutto

This is a creamy chicken, without the cream. Chicken Veronique has a very unique flavor from the grapes and tarragon. I like red grapes because they are a little sweeter. If you are using dried tarragon instead of fresh, remember to cut the tarragon down by half and add it when you add the stock. It is still delicious with the dried tarragon, but the fresh really is better.

Quinoa is a small grain with a nuttier flavor than rice, and it retains more texture than rice. The grapes and tarragon complement the nutty flavor of the quinoa very well.

The asparagus is served at room temperature so it can be made earlier in the day and refrigerated before bringing back to room temperature before serving. If you have a hard time finding or affording prosciutto, ham from the deli also works well for this recipe.

Chicken Veronique
Timing to table: 45 minutes
Serves 4

4 chicken breasts, boneless and skinless
1 small onion, finely diced
1 c seedless grapes, halved
1 T olive oil
1 c chicken stock
1 T water
1 T cornstarch
1 ½ T fresh tarragon
1 t salt
½ t pepper

In a large sauté pan over medium-high heat, heat olive oil. Season the chicken with salt and pepper. Add chicken to the pan and brown on both sides, about 5 minutes. Remove the chicken and reserve on the side. Lower the heat to medium and add onions to the pan. Sauté the onions about 5 minutes or until softened and lightly browned. Return chicken to the pan and add chicken stock. Simmer for 20 minutes or until the chicken is no longer pink. Remove the chicken and cover to keep warm. Add grapes and tarragon to pan juices. In a cup, combine water and cornstarch and whisk until smooth. Add cornstarch mixture to stock and grapes. When the gravy is thickened, return the chicken to the pan and coat with the gravy.

Quinoa
Timing to table: 30 minutes
Serves 4

1 c quinoa
2 c vegetable broth
½ t fresh tarragon
½ t salt

Rinse quinoa thoroughly in cold water. Add quinoa, salt and vegetable broth to a medium sauce pan. Bring to boil, reduce heat to low, then cover and simmer for 20 minutes. Add tarragon and cook an additional 5 minutes.

Roasted asparagus and prosciutto

Timing to table: 1 hour
Serves 4

1 lb asparagus
¼ lb prosciutto
1 T olive oil
½ t salt
¼ t pepper

Preheat oven to 425°. Toss asparagus with olive oil, salt and pepper. Roast the asparagus on a cookie sheet for 20 minutes or until tender. Transfer asparagus to a plate and allow to cool to room temperature. When cooled, wrap slices of prosciutto around bundles of 4 asparagus spears. Serve at room temperature.

Stuffed Chicken Breast, Tomato & Quinoa Salad, Roasted Cauliflower

This stuffed chicken has a definite Greek influence. The Kalamata olives and the sun-dried tomatoes really give the chicken breast a lot of flavor. I think the lemon juice at the end really brightens the flavor. When cooking the chicken breasts be careful not to overcook or they will be dry.

Quinoa is a wonderful grain that is very adaptable. I love it cold in salads because it can be made well in advance. I always rinse my quinoa, even when the package says it has already been rinsed, to prevent it from becoming bitter.

I like to roast most of my vegetables, and cauliflower is no exception. Roasting brings out a sweetness in the vegetables and gives them a crispy texture. Just a simple salt and pepper seasoning is all cauliflower needs to really bring out its flavor.

Stuffed chicken breast

Timing to table: 1 ½ hours
Serves 4

4 chicken breasts, boneless and skinless
2 oz sundried tomatoes packed in oil, chopped and oil reserved
¼ c Kalamata olives, chopped
1 red bell pepper
½ c chicken stock
1 t dried oregano
2 T lemon juice
¼ t garlic powder
½ t salt
¼ t pepper

Preheat the broiler. Place the red bell pepper on top of a sheet of foil under the broiler. Turn the pepper every 5 minutes, until charred. Place the pepper in a sealed container until cooled. When cooled, remove the skin and seeds from the pepper and dice.

Preheat the oven to 375°. In bowl combine red bell pepper, sun dried tomatoes, the reserved oil from the sundried tomatoes, olives, garlic powder and ½ teaspoon oregano. Slice a pocket into the chicken breasts. Season the chicken with ½ teaspoon oregano, salt and pepper. Stuff the tomato mixture into chicken breast and place the breasts into a roasting pan. Add chicken stock to the pan and roast 20 minutes or until juices run clear. Drizzle the lemon juice over the top of the chicken.

Tomato and quinoa salad

Timing to table: 1 ½ hour
Serves 4

1 c quinoa
3 tomatoes
2 scallions, sliced
2 c vegetable broth

Dressing

¼ c olive oil
2 T red wine vinegar
½ T honey
½ T Dijon mustard
¼ t dried thyme
¼ t dried oregano
¼ t salt
¼ t pepper

Rinse quinoa thoroughly in cold water. Combine quinoa and vegetable broth in a medium sauce pan. Bring the broth to a boil, reduce heat to low, cover and simmer for 25 minutes.

Whisk together vinegar, honey, mustard, olive oil, thyme and oregano. Chop 1 of the tomatoes. Add chopped tomato and scallions to the quinoa. Pour the dressing over the quinoa. Refrigerate the quinoa salad at least 1 hour.

Cut 2 tomatoes in half. Scoop out the inner flesh of the tomato halves. Fill tomato halves with the quinoa salad.

Roasted cauliflower
Timing to table: 30 minutes
Serves 4

1 lb cauliflower, sliced
1 T olive oil
½ t salt
¼ t pepper

Preheat the oven to 375°. Combine cauliflower with olive oil, salt and pepper. Roast in the oven for 25 minutes or until the stems are tender

Chicken Francaise, Rice Pilaf, Artichoke and Mushroom Salad

This is a simple chicken dish that has wonderful lemony flavor. Typical Chicken Francaise has a heavy egg breading, this version does not. I simply brown the chicken and create the Francaise sauce.

Rice pilaf is simply rice that has been sautéed in oil before adding stock. When browning the rice, be careful to avoid burning it. Once the rice starts to brown, it burns very quickly.

I love this recipe with the artichoke and mushroom salad, since the flavors are so complimentary. The longer you allow the mushrooms and artichoke to marinate in the dressing, the more flavorful the mushrooms become. I have also used this salad as part of an antipasto platter.

Chicken Francaise
Timing to table: 35 minutes
Serves 4

4 chicken breasts, boneless and skinless
1 clove garlic, minced
1 T olive oil
½ c white wine
1 c chicken stock
1 T water
1 T cornstarch
1 lemon, zest and juice
2 t dried parsley
½ t salt
½ t pepper

In a medium sauté pan, heat olive oil over medium-high heat. Add the chicken and brown on both sides, about 5 minutes. Add garlic and sauté 1 minute until golden. Add white wine to loosen the brown bits in the pan and reduce the wine until almost dry. Add chicken stock, parsley, salt, pepper and the zest from the lemon. Lower the heat to low, cover and simmer 20 minutes. When the chicken is no longer pink, add lemon juice to the sauce. In a cup, whisk together the cornstarch and water until smooth. Whisk the cornstarch mixture into the sauce.

Rice pilaf
Timing to table: 45 minutes
Serves 4

1 c basmati rice
1 small onion, diced
1 T olive oil
2 c chicken stock
1 t fresh thyme
½ t salt
¼ t pepper

In a medium sauce pan over medium heat, heat the olive oil. Add onions and sauté 10 minutes until golden brown. Add the rice and sauté until light brown, stirring constantly. Add chicken stock, salt, pepper and thyme. Bring to a boil, cover and reduce heat to low for 20 minutes or until rice is tender.

Artichoke and mushroom salad
Timing to table: 1 ½ hours
Serves 4

1 (14 oz) can artichoke hearts, drained
½ lb mushrooms, quartered
1 clove garlic, minced
¼ c olive oil
3 T lemon juice
1 t fresh parsley
1 t fresh thyme
½ t dried basil
½ t dried oregano
½ t salt
½ t pepper

Combine mushrooms and artichokes in a medium bowl. Whisk together olive oil, lemon juice, garlic, parsley, basil, oregano, thyme, salt and pepper. Pour the dressing over the mushrooms and artichokes. Cover and refrigerate for at least1 hour.

Roast Chicken and Vegetables

This was one of our go-to Sunday dinners when I was growing up. It is impressive enough for company without having to spend all day in the kitchen. Using chicken thighs instead of an entire roasting chicken reduces the cooking time considerably.

Roast chicken and vegetables

Timing to table: 1 hour
Serves 4

4 chicken thighs
4 small red potatoes, peeled and halved
4 carrots, peeled and cut in thirds
2 onions, halved
1 red bell pepper, quartered
1 green bell pepper, quartered
12 cloves garlic, peeled and whole
1 T vegetable oil
1 c chicken stock
1T water
1 T cornstarch
¾ t dried rosemary
1 t salt
½ t pepper

Preheat the oven to 425°. In a roasting pan toss potatoes, carrots, onions and garlic with vegetable oil, ½ teaspoon salt, ½ teaspoon rosemary and ¼ teaspoon pepper. Roast the vegetables for 20 minutes. Season the chicken thighs and bell peppers with ½ teaspoon salt, ¼ teaspoon rosemary and ¼ teaspoon pepper and add to the roasting pan with the vegetables. Roast an additional 25 minutes or until the chicken is cooked through.

Remove chicken and vegetables from the pan and pour out any grease from the pan. Place the roasting pan on the stovetop over high heat and add the chicken stock. Bring the stock to a boil to loosen browned bits. In a cup, combine water and cornstarch and mix until smooth. Whisk the cornstarch mixture into the chicken stock to thicken the gravy.

Chicken Marsala, Creamy Polenta, Arugula Salad

Chicken Marsala is a classic Italian dish that is actually very easy to make. I like to use a sweet Marsala wine rather than a dry Marsala. The cremini mushrooms in this dish really absorb the flavor of the chicken and wine. I like to serve this with the creamy polenta and then balance out the texture with some crunchy arugula.

When I make creamy polenta I use a rice milk, however, if you do not like rice milk or do not have easy access to it, use a little chicken stock instead and increase the margarine by 1 tablespoon. If you are using dried herbs instead of fresh, be sure to cut them back by half and add them with the cornmeal.

The dressing for the arugula is similar to the Italian dressing mix that comes in a pouch that is mixed at home. I often make up a batch of the dried herbs for the dressing and then just add the vinegar and oil whenever I need.

Chicken Marsala
Timing to table: 1 hour
Serves 4

4 chicken thighs, skinless
½ lb cremini mushrooms
1 T olive oil
½ cup sweet Marsala wine
½ cup chicken stock
1 T fresh basil, sliced
1 T fresh parsley, chopped
½ t salt
¼ t pepper

In a large skillet over medium-high heat, heat olive oil. Add chicken to the hot oil and sauté for 5 minutes on each side until golden. Remove the chicken and reserve on the side. Add the mushrooms, salt and pepper and sauté until browned, about 5 minutes. Add the Marsala to the pan and cook until almost evaporated. Return the chicken and add chicken stock to the pan. Bring the chicken stock to a boil, reduce heat to low and simmer for 30 minutes or until the chicken is no longer pink. Add the basil and parsley and cook another 1 minute.

Creamy polenta
Timing to table: 20 minutes
Serves 4

2/3 cup cornmeal
1 clove garlic, minced
1 T olive oil
2 T margarine
½ c rice milk
2 cups chicken stock
½ t fresh rosemary, chopped
½ t fresh thyme, chopped
½ t salt
¼ t pepper

In a large saucepan, heat olive oil over medium-high heat. Add the garlic and sauté for 1 minute. Add the chicken stock, rosemary, salt, pepper and thyme and bring to a boil. Reduce the heat to low and slowly whisk the cornmeal into the hot stock. Cook the cornmeal, stirring constantly, for 5 minutes until thickened and bubbly. Remove from the heat and add rice milk and margarine. Whisk smooth.

Arugula salad
Timing to table: 15 minutes
Serves 4

4 c arugula, washed
1 c cherry tomatoes, halved
1 scallion, sliced

Dressing

¼ c olive oil
2 T red wine vinegar
1 t dried oregano
1 t dried parsley
½ t garlic powder
½ t onion powder
¼ t dried basil
½ t salt
¼ t pepper

Combine arugula, tomatoes and scallions in a medium bowl. Whisk together vinegar, garlic powder, onion powder, oregano, basil, parsley, salt and pepper. Add the olive oil. Drizzle over the arugula and tomatoes.

Italian Chicken, Roasted Rosemary Potatoes, Tomato Salad

This tangy chicken recipe is loaded with capers and red and green peppers. When the chicken is done, you will notice that the chicken and peppers have absorbed most of the juices from the pan, which leaves the peppers and chicken extremely tender and moist.

I like the combination of the crispy potatoes with the tender chicken and peppers. These potatoes have a great crispy coating and lots of flavor. I have found turning the potatoes only once after 20 minutes - and then not again - helps keep the potatoes from sticking.

Because the chicken has more complex flavors, I really like the idea of a simpler salad. This tomato salad has wonderful simple flavors of balsamic vinegar and basil. The red onions, which will mellow as they sit in the vinegar, add just a little bite.

Italian chicken
Timing to table: 1 ½ hours
Serves 4

4 chicken thighs, skinless
1 red bell pepper, sliced
1 green bell pepper, sliced
1 onion, sliced
2 cloves garlic, minced
2 T capers
1 T olive oil
¾ c chicken stock
1 t dried thyme
1 t dried oregano
½ t salt
½ t pepper

In medium skillet over medium-high heat, heat olive oil. Season the chicken with ¼ teaspoon salt and ¼ teaspoon pepper. Brown the chicken 5 minutes on each side in the hot oil. Remove the chicken and reserve on the side. Add the bell peppers and onions and sauté until slightly browned, about 5 minutes. Add the garlic. Return the chicken to the pan and add the capers, thyme, oregano, ¼ teaspoon salt, ¼ teaspoon pepper and the chicken stock. Bring the stock to a boil, reduce the heat to medium low and cook uncovered for 45 minutes, until the chicken is cooked through.

Roasted rosemary potatoes
Timing to table: 40 minutes
Serves 4

4 Yukon Gold potatoes, cubed
1 T olive oil
¼ t garlic powder
1 t dried rosemary, chopped
½ t salt
¼ t pepper

Preheat the oven to 425°. Combine potatoes with olive oil, salt, pepper, rosemary and garlic powder. Place the potatoes on a cookie sheet. Roast for 30 minutes turning once.

Tomato salad

Timing to table: 10 minutes
Serves 4

2 large tomatoes, sliced into wedges
1 small red onion, thinly sliced
1 T olive oil
1 T balsamic vinegar
1 T fresh basil, sliced
½ t salt
¼ t pepper

Combine tomatoes and onions in a medium bowl. Whisk the vinegar with olive oil, basil, salt and pepper. Toss tomatoes and onion with the dressing.

Chicken Cacciatore, Sautéed Polenta, Roasted Fennel

Chicken cacciatore is a red sauce with mushrooms and peppers. I like my cacciatore sauce to be very thick. If you like a thinner sauce, simply increase the amount of water you add. The sauce from the cacciatore goes wonderfully with the polenta and the roasted fennel. I actually prefer the sauce on top both the fennel and polenta.

Sautéed polenta is just polenta that has been cooked, chilled and then sautéed crispy. I like to make sure that the polenta is in a thin layer in the pan when I chill it. This ensures that the polenta will be very crispy when it's sautéed.

Fennel is an aromatic vegetable that has a licorice flavor. Since fennel gets less flavorful the more it is cooked, when I roast it I make sure it still has a little crunch. Overcooking the fennel can cause it to be bland.

Chicken cacciatore
Timing to table: 1 hour
Serves 4

4 chicken thighs, skinless
1 green bell pepper, diced into 1 inch pieces
½ lb mushrooms, sliced
1 onion, diced into 1 inch pieces
2 cloves garlic, minced
2 T tomato paste
1 (14-oz) can crushed tomatoes
1 T olive oil
½ c water
1 t dried basil
1 t dried parsley
½ t dried oregano
1 t salt
½ t pepper

In large skillet, heat olive oil over medium-high heat. Season the chicken with ½ teaspoon salt and ¼ teaspoon pepper. Brown the chicken in the hot oil 5 minutes on each side. Remove the chicken and reserve on the side. Lower the heat to medium and add the onions, bell peppers and mushrooms. Sauté the vegetables about 10 minutes or until golden. Add garlic, tomato paste, basil, parsley, ½ teaspoon salt and ¼ teaspoon pepper. Sauté another 3 minutes and add the canned tomatoes and water. Return the chicken to the skillet. Bring the sauce to a boil, reduce heat to low and simmer 30 minutes or until chicken is cooked through.

Sautéed polenta
Timing to table: 1 ½ hours
Serves 4

2/3 c cornmeal
½ small red onion, finely chopped
1 cloves garlic, finely minced
2 T olive oil
2 c chicken stock
½ t salt
¼ t pepper

In a large saucepan over medium heat, heat 1 tablespoon of olive oil. Add the garlic and onions and sauté for 15 minute. Add the chicken stock and bring to a boil. Lower the heat to low and whisk the cornmeal into the hot stock. Cook over low heat, stirring constantly, for a 5 minutes, until thickened and bubbly. Pour into a 9 by 13 inch pan and refrigerate until firm, about 30 minutes.

Cut the chilled polenta into 8 squares. In a large sauté pan over medium-high heat, heat 1 tablespoon olive oil. Sauté the polenta squares 5 minutes per side.

Roasted fennel
Timing to table: 25 minutes
Serves 4

2 fennel bulbs, sliced 1 inch thick, fronds and core removed
1 T olive oil
½ t dried oregano
½ t salt
¼ t pepper

Preheat the oven to 375°. Mix fennel, olive oil, salt, pepper and oregano. Place the fennel on a cookie sheet. Roast 20 minutes or until barely tender.

Chicken in Wine

This is my version of Coq au Vin. I like using white wine instead of the classic red because it keeps the chicken from changing color. When making this dish, take the extra time to really cook each item separately. It really elevates the flavor of the entire meal.

Chicken in wine
Timing to table: 2 hours
Serves 4

4 chicken thighs, skinless
4 slices bacon, diced
8 medium carrots, peeled and quartered
1 medium yellow onions, diced
2 cloves garlic, minced
1 pound frozen pearl onions, thawed
1 pound mushrooms, thickly sliced
2 large red potatoes, peeled and thickly sliced
1 c white wine
2 c chicken stock
1 t fresh thyme
1 t salt
½ t pepper

Preheat the oven to 350°. Heat a large Dutch oven over medium-high heat. Add the bacon and cook until crispy. Remove the bacon with a slotted spoon to a large plate. Season the chicken with ½ teaspoon salt and ¼ teaspoon pepper. Brown the chicken in the hot bacon fat about 5 minutes per side. Remove the chicken to another plate. Reduce the heat to medium and add the pearl onions. Cook 15 minutes and remove the browned onions. Reserve the pearl onions on the plate with the bacon. Add the mushrooms and brown, about 15 minutes. Remove the mushrooms and reserve with the pearl onions. Add the carrots. Brown the carrots for 15 minutes, then add the diced onion. Sauté the diced onion until softened then add the garlic. Add the wine and scrape the bottom of the pan. When the wine is reduced by half, add the chicken stock, potatoes, thyme, ½ teaspoon salt, and ¼ teaspoon pepper. Return the chicken to the pot.

Bring the stock to a boil, cover and place the Dutch oven in the oven for about 30 minutes or until the meat and vegetables are very tender when pierced with a fork. Remove the lid and add the pearl onions, bacon and mushrooms back in. Cook another 15 minutes to reduce the juices.

Jambalaya

There are two basic types of jambalaya, Cajun and Creole. The biggest difference between the two is the addition of tomatoes in the Creole version. This is a mild Cajun recipe. By changing the type of smoked sausage and adding more cayenne, you can increase the heat to your own liking.

Jambalaya
Timing to table: 2 hours
Serves 4

1 lb smoked sausage, thickly sliced
2 chicken thighs, boneless, skinless and cubed
1 onion, diced
1 carrot, peeled and diced
2 ribs celery, diced
1 green bell pepper, diced
1 c rice
2 ½ c chicken stock
1 t dried thyme
1 t dried basil
1 t dried parsley
1 t salt
¼ t pepper
¼ t cayenne

In heavy skillet over medium-high heat, brown the sausage and chicken. Remove the meat from the pan and reserve on the side. Add the onions, carrots, celery, and green pepper. Sauté for 15 minutes or until golden brown. Add the salt, pepper, cayenne, basil, thyme and parsley to the sautéed vegetables. Return the chicken and sausage to the pan and add the chicken stock. Bring the stock to a boil, reduce the heat to low and simmer for 30 minutes. Add rice and simmer for another 30 minutes.

Stuffed Cornish Hens, Broccoli Rabe

Cornish hens are as easy to cook as chicken, yet they look very elegant. I like the contrast of the wild rice as a stuffing. The juices from the Cornish hens run into the wild rice stuffing and really add to its flavor.

Broccoli rabe is similar to broccoli with a slightly more bitter flavor. Boiling the broccoli rabe first removes that bitterness. A quick toss in the flavored oil really compliments the broccoli rabe's flavor.

Cornish hens
Timing to table: 2 hours
Serves 4

4 Cornish game hens
1 c wild rice
½ small onion, chopped
1 T vegetable oil
2 c chicken stock
1 teaspoon salt
½ t pepper

In a medium saucepan over medium heat, heat vegetable oil. Add the onions, and sauté 5 minutes or until softened. Add the wild rice and coat with the oil. Add in the chicken stock, and ½ teaspoon salt. Bring to a boil, reduce heat to low, cover, and simmer 45 minutes until the rice is tender.

Preheat oven to 400°. Season the Cornish game hens inside and out with ½ teaspoon salt and pepper. Stuff the hens with the rice mixture. Place the hens breast side up on a rack in a roasting pan. Cook about 1 hour or until the hens are no longer pink and the juices run clear.

Broccoli rabe
Timing to table: 20 minutes
Serves 4

1 lb broccoli rabe,
3 cloves garlic, sliced thin
1 T olive oil
1 qt water
1 t salt
Dash red pepper flakes

Bring a large pot of water to a boil. Add the broccoli rabe and salt. Boil for 5 minute or until stems are tender. Drain the broccoli rabe.

Over medium high heat, add olive oil to a large sauté pan. Add the garlic to the pan. Once the garlic is brown, add the broccoli rabe and red pepper flakes. Toss the broccoli rabe in the oil and garlic for 1 minute.

Roast Turkey, Mashed Sweet Potato, Green Bean Casserole

Cooking turkey can be a pain, which is probably why many people eat it just once a year. This recipe is easy, the turkey is moist and delicious, and it can be prepared well in advance. This turkey is different from most, since it is not served with its skin on. I make the turkey early in the day, slice it and then reheat it in the gravy. I do this for two reasons. First, I don't have to worry about whether or not the breast will be dry, since I will be reheating it in gravy. Second, I don't have to worry about the timing. I just take out the turkey whenever it is done, then I simply reheat for 30 minutes and serve.

Turkey almost "needs" sweet potatoes to accompany it. These potatoes are mashed smooth with a bruleed sugar topping. I like the individual ramekins for serving, although I have used a single casserole dish.

Green bean casserole is a traditional turkey side dish. I have simply made a dairy-free cream of mushroom soup for these. Then I top the dish with oven baked onion slices.

Roast turkey
Timing to table: 3 hours
Serves 8

6 lb turkey
¼ c fresh sage
½ t garlic powder
1 t salt
½ t pepper
5 T cornstarch
5 T water

Preheat oven to 375°. Carefully loosen the skin of the turkey by sliding your hand between the skin and the meat. Season the turkey under the skin with salt, pepper and garlic powder. Stuff the sage into the turkey cavity. Roast the turkey for 1 ½ hours or until the breast registers 165°. Allow the turkey to cool for at least 15 minutes, then remove the skin and carve.

On the stovetop bring the turkey drippings to a boil. In a cup, whisk cornstarch and water together until smooth. Whisk cornstarch into the turkey drippings. Return sliced turkey to the pan and coat with the gravy. Allow turkey and gravy to cool to room temperature and refrigerate.

Thirty minutes before serving, return the turkey to a 400° oven until heated.

Mashed sweet potatoes
Timing to table: 20 minutes
Serves 4

3 medium sweet potatoes
2 T margarine
2 T brown sugar
½ t salt
¼ t pepper

Microwave the sweet potatoes for 10 minutes or until very tender. Slice sweet potatoes in half and scoop the flesh out into a medium bowl. Add margarine, salt and pepper. Beat the sweet potatoes until smooth. Spoon potatoes into ramekins and sprinkle with brown sugar. Broil 3 minutes or until sugar gets brown and crusty.

Green beans casserole
Timing to table: 1 hour
Serves 4

1 lb green beans, cleaned
½ lb mushrooms, diced
1 large onion, thickly sliced
1 medium onion, diced
1 clove garlic, minced
2 T olive oil
1 c rice milk
1 c chicken stock
7 T water
5 T cornstarch
½ t dried thyme
¼ t nutmeg
½ t salt
¼ t pepper

Preheat the oven to 400°. In a small bowl combine 1 sliced onion, 2 tablespoons cornstarch and 2 tablespoons water. Coat a cookie sheet with 1 tablespoon olive oil. Lay onions in a single layer on a cookie sheet and roast 20 minutes or until crisped.

In a covered microwavable bowl, add green beans and 2 tablespoons water. Microwave the beans on high for 7 minutes or until tender. Drain and reserve the beans on the side.

In a medium sauce pan, heat 1 tablespoon olive oil. Sauté diced onions and mushrooms until golden, about 15 minutes. Add salt, pepper, nutmeg and thyme. Stir in the rice milk and chicken stock. In a cup, whisk 3 tablespoons water and 3 tablespoons cornstarch together until smooth. Add cornstarch mixture to the rice milk. Stir in the cooked green beans.

Transfer the green beans to a casserole dish and top with a layer of the crispy onions. Bake for 30 minutes.

Lamb

Shepherd's Pie

Shepherd's pie is a rich dish with lamb and vegetables cooked in a flavorful sauce and topped with mashed potatoes. I am a big fan of one pot meals, so I add more vegetables to my shepherd's pie than is traditional. If you are not a fan of lamb or if it is cost prohibitive, simply use ground beef.

Shepherd's pie
Timing to table: 1 ½ hours
Serves 4

1.5 lb ground lamb
4 Russet potatoes, peeled and cubed
1 medium onion, diced
6 mushrooms, diced
3 cloves garlic
2 carrots, peeled and diced
½ c frozen peas
½ c green beans
1 T tomato paste
2 T margarine
½ c chicken stock
2 T red wine
2 qts water
¼ c rice milk
1 T fresh rosemary, chopped
1 T fresh thyme, chopped
1 T *Lea and Perrins* Worcestershire sauce
2 t salt
½ t pepper

In large sauté pan over medium high heat, brown the ground lamb for about 5 minutes. Drain all but 1 tablespoon of fat from pan. Add the onion, mushrooms and carrots. Sauté about 10 minutes or until lightly browned then add 2 cloves of minced garlic, rosemary and thyme. When the garlic starts to brown add frozen peas, green bean and tomato paste. Deglaze the pan with red wine and cook until the wine reduces completely down. Add the chicken stock, Worcestershire sauce, 1 teaspoon salt and ¼ teaspoon pepper. Bring to a boil and reduce heat. Simmer ½ hour or until chicken stock has been reduced to 1 tablespoon.

In a large sauce pan add potatoes and cover with cold water. Add 1 whole garlic clove to water. Bring the water to a boil and add 1 teaspoon salt to the pot. Reduce the heat to medium and cook for 25 minutes until potatoes are tender. Drain the potatoes and discard the garlic clove. Mash the potatoes with margarine until smooth. Beat in rice milk. Add ¼ teaspoon pepper.

Preheat oven to 375°. Transfer the lamb mixture to a casserole dish. Top with the potatoes. Bake the casserole for 30 minutes or until the potatoes are browned.

Leg of Lamb, Double Baked Potato, Roasted Butternut Squash

I make this lamb every year for the holidays. The marinade mellows the flavor of the lamb just slightly. I prefer the semi-boneless roasts for easier carving. Remember, while the lamb is resting after roasting, the temperature will continue to rise another ten degrees.

These double baked potatoes are a classic pairing of bacon, potatoes and scallions. They are rich and creamy with a nice crispy top. The potatoes can be made earlier in the day and refrigerated. When reheating in the oven, bake for 30 minutes instead of 15.

Roasted butternut squash has a similar flavor to sweet potatoes. These are baked with brown sugar until lightly browned and very tender. Make sure you use a large heavy knife when cutting the squash, since butternut squash is very dense when raw.

Leg of lamb
Timing to table: 24 hours
Serves 8

5 lb leg of lamb, semi-boneless
6 cloves garlic, minced
2 T olive oil
2 T fresh rosemary, minced
1 T salt
1 t pepper.

Mix together olive oil, rosemary, garlic, salt and pepper and massage into the lamb. Cover the lamb and marinate overnight in the refrigerator.

Preheat the oven to 325°. Uncover the lamb and roast for 1 ½ hours or until it reaches 125° for medium rare. Allow to rest 15 minutes before carving.

Double baked potato
Timing to table: 1 ½ hours
Serves 4

4 large Russet potatoes, scrubbed
3 slices bacon
2 scallions, sliced
3 T margarine
½ c rice milk
¼ t salt
½ t pepper

Preheat the oven to 375°. Bake the potatoes for 1 hour.

In a large skillet over medium-high heat, brown the bacon. Place the bacon on paper towels until cool.

Allow potatoes to cool slightly, cut off the top of the potatoes and scoop out the flesh being careful not to break the skin. Add 2 tablespoons margarine, rice milk, salt, and pepper to potatoes and mash until smooth. Crumble the bacon and add to the potatoes along with the scallions and mix well. Spoon the potato mixture back into the potato skins and top with the remaining margarine. Bake 15 more minutes or until the tops begin to brown

Roasted butternut squash
Timing to table: 50 minutes
Serves 4

1 butternut squash
1 T olive oil
1 T brown sugar
½ t salt
¼ t pepper

Preheat the oven to 375°. Peel the squash and cut in half. Remove the seeds and cut the butternut squash into 1 inch cubes. Combine the squash with olive oil, sugar, salt and pepper. Bake 40 minutes or until tender and golden brown.

Beef

Chili

This is my version of Texas chili, although I like the addition of beans. I don't have any vegetables in this recipe, just meat, beans and sauce. The chili should be thick and the meat very tender. If the chili begins to stick to the bottom of the pot, add two tablespoons of water as necessary. This chili is not so spicy that you cannot taste the flavors of the chili. I often double or triple this recipe for large crowds.

Chili

Timing to table: 3 hours
Serves 4

2 lb bottom round beef roast, cut into 1 inch cubes
1 (15-oz) can kidney beans, drained
3 c beef stock
1 c tomato sauce
3 T chili powder
1 T cumin
1 t onion powder
1 t garlic powder
1 t dried oregano
½ t brown sugar

In a large stock pot over medium-high heat, brown the beef on all sides. Add the beef stock, tomato sauce, cumin, oregano, brown sugar, onion powder, chili powder, and garlic powder. Bring to a boil, reduce heat to low and simmer 2 hours, stirring often to prevent the chili from burning on the bottom. Add the beans and cook an additional 30 minutes.

Tacos, Black Bean Salad

I love the ease of tacos. My family, however, has issues with most of the packaged taco seasoning mixes. I finally gave up and decided to make my own, and found that making my own seasoning mix is very easy and inexpensive.

This bean salad is a wonderful side for tacos. I prefer to top my taco with the salad, which has beans and corn and a salsa-like flavor. In fact, my kids like the black bean salad as an appetizer dip with tortilla chips. I have added a jalapeño pepper to this recipe for a spicy variation.

Tacos
Timing to table: 1 hour
Serves 4

1 lb ground beef
8 taco shells
½ head lettuce, sliced
1 tomato, diced
1 avocado, diced
1 c water
1 T chili powder
1 ½ t cumin
½ t paprika
¼ t garlic powder
¼ t onion powder
¼ t red pepper flakes
¼ t oregano
¼ t salt
½ t pepper

Over medium-high heat, brown beef in a medium sauté pan. Stir chili powder, cumin, red pepper flakes, salt, paprika, pepper, garlic powder and onion powder into browned beef. Add water, reduce the heat to low and simmer 30 minutes or until all the water has evaporated. Fill taco shells with beef mixture and top with lettuce, tomato and avocado.

Black bean salad
Timing to table: 1 ½ hours
Serves 4

1 (15-oz) can black beans, drained
1 c frozen corn, thawed
1 small red onion, diced
2 tomatoes, diced
1 clove garlic, minced
2 t chipotle chilies, minced
1 T olive oil
2 T lime juice
2 t red wine vinegar
2 T fresh cilantro

½ t cumin
½ t salt

In a medium bowl, combine beans, corn, onions, tomatoes and garlic. Whisk together lime juice, vinegar, salt, cumin, chipotle chilies, and cilantro. Slowly whisk in the olive oil. Drizzle the dressing over the beans and mix carefully. Refrigerate for at least 1 hour before serving.

Spaghetti Squash and Meatballs, Endive Salad

I love spaghetti squash instead of pasta with marinara sauce, and it makes a great alternative for gluten-free diets. Spaghetti squash looks like most winter squash when raw, but once it's cooked, it shreds resembling spaghetti. The sweetness of the squash cuts any of the bitterness of the canned tomatoes in the sauce.

The meatballs are more fragile than if they were made with eggs, which is why I bake them in the oven and then transfer them to the sauce once they are brown and firm. I use *Rice Chex* cereal in them instead of bread crumbs.

Endives are a crunchy salad green that works great with the creamy avocado. I like pairing the endives and avocado with a honey mustard vinaigrette.

Spaghetti squash
Timing to table: 1 ½ hours
Serves 4

2 spaghetti squash
1 large onion, diced
2 cloves garlic, minced
1 carrot, diced
1 (28-oz) can crushed tomatoes
3 T tomato paste
1 T olive oil
1 c water
1 T dried basil
1 t dried oregano
1 t dried parsley
½ t dried rosemary
½ t pepper
½ t salt

Preheat the oven to 375°. Cut the spaghetti squash in half and remove the seeds. Place the squash on a cookie sheet cut side down and roast for 1 hour or until tender. Allow to cool a few minutes then with a fork, scrape the flesh out of the squash. Reserve the squash on the side.

In skillet, heat olive oil over medium heat. Add onions and carrots and sauté 15 minutes until tender. Add garlic and tomato paste and cook for 2 minutes. Add crushed tomatoes, basil, water, oregano, rosemary, salt, pepper and parsley. Bring sauce to a boil; reduce heat to low and simmer partially covered for 1 hour. Mix the spaghetti squash into the sauce.

Meatballs
Timing to table: 1 hour
Serves 4

1 lb ground beef
½ c *Rice Chex* cereal
1 small onion, grated
1 clove garlic, grated
½ c beef stock
1 t dried parsley

1 t dried basil
½ t salt
¼ t pepper

Preheat the oven to 375°. In a large bowl, combine beef stock and *Rice Chex*. Allow to soak 30 minutes. Add the ground beef, grated onion and garlic, parsley, basil, salt and pepper and mix together. Form into balls and place on a cookie sheet. Bake meatballs in the oven 20 minutes or until browned. Add the meatballs to the above sauce before serving.

Endive salad
Timing to table: 10 minutes
Serves 4

2 heads endive, halved and cored
2 avocados, sliced
1/4 c olive oil
2 T red wine vinegar
1 T honey Dijon mustard
½ t dried parsley
½ t dried basil
½ t salt
¼ t pepper

Whisk together the mustard, vinegar, salt, parsley, basil and pepper. Slowly whisk in the olive oil. Arrange the endive and avocado on your serving plate and drizzle the dressing over the top.

Stuffed Peppers, Eggplant

Stuffed peppers are a very versatile dish. You can substitute or add different vegetables or ground meats to the peppers to suit your tastes. If you are vegetarian, simply replace the beef with mushrooms and cooked beans.

I was trying to cook eggplant without needing to use a lot of oil and found that broiling is a great option. Eggplant can really soak up oil when trying to sauté it. Broiling however, allows you to control the amount of oil you use. I just coat the slices with the oil and broil them.

Stuffed peppers
Timing to table: 1 hour
Serves 4

2 lb ground beef
1 c white rice
4 bell peppers, cut in half and de-seeded
1 medium onion, diced
1 clove garlic, minced
3 oz green olive, halved
1 (28-oz) can tomato sauce
2½ c beef stock
2 t dried basil
1 t dried oregano
1 t salt
½ t pepper

In medium sauté pan over medium heat, brown the ground beef. Drain the fat from the beef and add onions and garlic. Cook 5 minutes and add the rice and beef stock. Add 1 teaspoon basil, ½ teaspoon salt, and ¼ teaspoon pepper. Cook 20 minutes or until the rice is tender. Remove the beef and rice from the heat and add olives.

In a small bowl, mix tomato sauce with 1 teaspoon basil, oregano, ½ teaspoon salt and ¼ teaspoon pepper.

Preheat the oven to 350°. Place bell pepper halves into a casserole dish. Spoon the beef and rice mixture into the pepper halves. Pour the tomato sauce over the peppers. Bake for 30 minutes.

Eggplant
Timing to table: 15 minutes
Serves 4

1 large eggplant, sliced ½ inch thick
1 T olive oil
½ t dried oregano
½ t salt
¼ t pepper

Preheat the broiler. Brush the eggplant with olive oil and sprinkle with salt, pepper, and oregano. Broil the eggplant 3 minutes per side.

Beef Stew

This is a extremely flavorful beef stew. The flavor of the stew varies greatly depending on the type of paprika you prefer to use. I like a sweet paprika, but my sons prefer a smoked paprika.

Beef stew
Timing to table: 3 hours
Serves 4

1 ½ lb beef, cut into 1 inch cubes
4 slices bacon, diced
2 medium onions, diced
3 garlic cloves, minced
2 red bell peppers
3 large red potatoes, cut into 2 inch cubes
1 (15-oz) can diced tomatoes, drained
2 c frozen green beans
2 c beef stock
2 T water
2 T cornstarch
1T paprika
1 t caraway seeds
1 t salt
¼ t pepper

Preheat the broiler. Place the red peppers on top of aluminum foil under the broiler. Turn the peppers every 5 minutes, until charred. Place the peppers in a sealed container until cooled. When cooled, remove the skin and seeds from the peppers and dice.

Over medium heat in a large skillet, fry bacon about 5 minutes until crispy. Remove the bacon and reserve on the side. Season the beef with salt and pepper and add the beef to the hot bacon fat. Brown the beef evenly on all sides. Add the onions, garlic, roasted peppers, paprika and caraway seeds. Sauté the vegetables 5 minutes or until the onions begin to brown. Add the tomatoes, green beans and beef stock. Bring to a boil, reduce heat to low, cover and simmer for 1 hour, stirring occasionally. Add the potatoes and cook an additional 30 minutes. In a cup, whisk together water and cornstarch until smooth. Slowly whisk into boiling stew.

Beef Bourguignon

Beef bourguignon is simply a fancy beef stew. The vegetables are browned separately, and then they are combined to make this wonderful stew. Typically, more wine is added to beef bourguignon, but my kids aren't crazy about the strong flavor, so I add a combination of wine and stock. Make sure the wine you add is to your taste to drink. I don't cook with wine that I wouldn't drink by the glass. I also like adding potatoes to this dish so the entire meal is in one pot.

Beef Bourguignon
Timing to table: 2 ½ hours
Serves 4

2 ½ lb bottom round beef roast, cut into 2 ½ inch cubes
4 slices bacon, diced
1 pound frozen pearl onions, thawed
1 pound mushrooms, thickly sliced
8 medium carrots, peeled and quartered
1 medium onions, diced
2 cloves garlic, minced
2 large red potatoes, peeled and thickly sliced
1c red wine
2 c beef stock
1 T tomato paste
½ t dried thyme
1 t salt
½ t pepper

Preheat the oven to 350°. Heat a large Dutch oven over medium-high heat. Add the bacon and cook until crispy. Remove the bacon with a slotted spoon to a large plate. Season the beef with ½ teaspoon salt and ¼ teaspoon pepper. Brown the beef in the hot bacon fat about 5 minutes per side. Remove the beef to another plate. Reduce the heat to medium and add the pearl onions. Cook 15 minutes and then remove the browned onions. Reserve the onions on the side with the bacon. Add the mushrooms and brown them, another 15 minutes. Remove the mushrooms and reserve with the pearl onions. Add the carrots and brown the carrots for 15 minutes, then add the diced onion. Sauté the diced onion until softened then add the garlic. Add the wine and tomato paste and scrape the bottom of the pan. When the wine is reduced by half, add the beef stock, potatoes, thyme, ½ teaspoon salt, and ¼ teaspoon pepper. Return the beef back to the pot.

Bring the stock to a boil, cover and place the Dutch oven in the oven for about 45 minutes or until the meat and vegetables are very tender when pierced with a fork. Remove the lid and add the pearl onions, bacon and mushrooms back into the pot. Cook another 15 minutes to thicken the gravy.

Round Steak, Parsley Potatoes, Cucumber Salad

This was one of my grandfather's favorite recipes. The round steak has a very unique flavor due to the nutmeg, and it complements the boiled potatoes.

The boiled potatoes in this recipe are just lightly flavored with margarine and parsley. They soak up the gravy from the round steak.

Traditionally, cucumber salad is made with mayonnaise, but this dressing has all the same flavors. The cucumber salad flavors blend and mellow the longer it rests. I usually make this in the morning of the day I plan to serve.

Round steak

Timing to table: 1 ½ hours
Serves 4

2 lb round steak, cut into 2 inch cubes
1 large onion, sliced
2 T olive oil
1 c beef stock
¼ c cornstarch
½ t nutmeg
1 t salt
½ t pepper

Combine cornstarch, salt, pepper and nutmeg. Dredge the steak in the cornstarch mixture, leaving a heavy coating of cornstarch. In a medium skillet over medium-high heat, heat olive oil. Brown the steak well, about 8 minutes, on both sides. Remove the steak and reserve on the side. Add onions and sauté 5 minutes until softened. Return the steak to the skillet and add beef stock. Bring the stock to a boil, reduce heat to low, cover and simmer 1 hour or until meat is very tender.

Parsley potatoes

Timing to table: 25 minutes
Serves 4

4 medium red potatoes, peeled and diced
2 qts water
1 T margarine
1 T fresh parsley, chopped
1 t salt
¼ t pepper

In a medium sauce pan, bring potatoes and water to a boil over high heat. Add salt, reduce heat to medium and cook until the potatoes are tender, about 20 minutes. Drain the potatoes. Carefully toss the potatoes with margarine, parsley and pepper.

Cucumbers salad
Timing to table: 1 ½ hours
Serves 4

2 large cucumbers, very thinly sliced
1 small red onion, very thinly sliced
¼ c olive oil
1 T red wine vinegar
1 t mustard
1 T fresh dill
½ t salt
¼ t pepper

Whisk mustard and vinegar with salt and pepper in a medium bowl. Slowly whisk in olive oil. Add cucumbers and onions. Top with dill and mix well. Refrigerate for at least 1 hour.

Beef with Mushrooms, Baked Brown Rice, Spinach Salad

I was craving beef stroganoff one night and came up with this recipe, really hits all the flavors I was looking for in the stroganoff. I like to use a variety of mushrooms for different tastes and textures.

Baked rice is a simple way to cook rice. The rice gets slightly crispy around the edges and fluffy in the center. I don't like to add much extra flavor to the rice, since I pour the sauce of the beef with mushrooms over the top of it.

The spinach salad is a very classic recipe with mushrooms, red onions and a bacon dressing. The warm dressing wilts the spinach ever so slightly.

Beef with mushrooms
Timing to table: 45 minutes
Serves 4

2 lb sirloin steak,
1 medium onion, chopped
1 lb mushrooms, sliced
3 cloves garlic, chopped
2 T vegetable oil
1 c beef stock
1 t Dijon mustard
1 t fresh thyme
½ t salt
¼ t pepper

Season the steak with salt and pepper. In a large skillet over medium-high heat, heat 1 tablespoon of vegetable oil. Add the steak to the hot oil and cook 5 minutes per side. Remove the beef and tent with foil.

Add the mushrooms and onions to the skillet and cook 10 minutes or until softened. Add the garlic and thyme and cook another 2 minutes. Whisk the beef stock and mustard into the skillet and boil 5 minutes until reduced by half. Slice the steak and return the steak to the pan for 1 minute.

Baked brown rice
Timing to table: 1 ½ hours
Serves 4

1 c brown rice
2½ c beef stock

Preheat the oven to 375°. In a small sauce pan bring the beef stock to a boil. Stir in the rice. Transfer the rice to an 8 inch casserole dish. Cover the casserole dish tightly with foil. Bake for 1 hour.

Spinach salad
Timing to table: 20 minutes
Serves 4

1 lb fresh spinach, washed
1 lb bacon, diced
1 small red onion, sliced
¼ lb mushrooms, sliced
3 T balsamic vinegar
1 t sugar
1 t Dijon mustard

In a salad bowl, layer spinach, mushrooms and onion. In a medium skillet over medium heat, brown the bacon and reserve on the side. Reserve 3 T of bacon fat and combine with vinegar, sugar and Dijon mustard. Pour the dressing over the spinach while still warm. Top with crumbled bacon.

Marinated Skirt Steak, Creamed Corn, Mashed Cauliflower

I find that skirt steak is very tough if it is not marinated. This marinade tenderizes and flavors the skirt steak. I like my steak medium rare, but adjust the temperature and cooking time of your steak to suit your tastes. When you carve skirt steak, be sure you are cutting against the grain.

Since we're dairy-free, the creamed corn is not really creamed; it simply uses the juices from scraping the corn husks, which creates a wonderful creamy dish.

Mashed cauliflower is a fun way to serve cauliflower. Unlike potatoes, cauliflower can be mashed in the food processor for a really smooth and creamy vegetable. My husband doesn't ordinarily like cauliflower, but he loves this recipe. If you don't have a food processor, a hand mixer also works very well.

Marinated skirt steak
Timing to table: 2 ½ hours
Serves 4

2 lbs skirt steak
2 cloves garlic, minced
1 small onion, minced
½ c olive oil
¼ c lime juice
2 T brown sugar
1 t cumin
1 t dried rosemary
1 t salt
½ t pepper

Whisk together oil, cumin, garlic, rosemary, minced onion, lime juice, brown sugar, pepper, and salt. Pour marinade over steak. Cover and refrigerate for at least 2 hours.

Preheat the broiler. Broil the steak 4 minutes per side for medium rare. Allow the skirt steak to rest 5 minutes then slice against the grain.

Creamed corn
Timing to table: 15 minutes
Serves 4

4 ears of fresh corn
1 T margarine
½ c water
½ t salt
¼ t pepper

Cut corn off the cob into a medium sauté pan. Scrape the back of the knife down the cob to extract the juices from the corn cob. Add the corn cob juices to the pan with the corn. Add water, margarine, salt, and pepper to the pan. Bring the water to a boil over medium heat. Cook for 10 minutes, stirring frequently, until the water has evaporated.

Mashed cauliflower
Timing to table: 15 minutes
Serves 4

1 lb cauliflower, cut into florets
1 T margarine
2 T water
¼ c rice milk
¼ t garlic powder
½ t salt
¼ t pepper

In a covered microwavable bowl, combine cauliflower, garlic powder and water. Steam the cauliflower in the microwave for 10 minutes, or until very tender. Drain the cauliflower well. Place the cauliflower in a food processor with the margarine, rice milk, salt and pepper. Process for 3 minutes until the cauliflower is very smooth.

Pot Roast

This is a wonderful classic pot roast. Browning the meat and vegetables first adds an additional layer of flavor. However, in a pinch I have skipped this step and gone directly into the oven.

Pot roast

Timing to table: 2 ½ hours
Serves 4

3 lb chuck roast
1 large onion, quartered with root end attached
4 medium red potatoes, peeled and quartered
8 carrots, peeled and cut in thirds
½ lb mushrooms, de-stemmed
2 T vegetable oil
2 c + 2 T water
2 T cornstarch
1 t dried thyme
½ t garlic powder
2 t salt
½ t pepper

Preheat the oven to 350°. Season the meat with ¼ teaspoon garlic powder, 1 teaspoon salt and ¼ teaspoon pepper. In a Dutch oven over medium-high heat, sear meat on both sides. Remove the meat and reserve on the side. Reduce the heat to medium and add vegetable oil. Season the onions, potatoes, carrots and mushrooms with 1 teaspoon thyme, 1 teaspoon salt, ¼ teaspoon pepper and ¼ teaspoon garlic powder and add to the Dutch oven. Sauté the vegetables for 10 minutes or until they begin to brown. Return the meat to the Dutch oven and add 2 cups of water. Bring the water to a boil and roast covered in the oven for 2 hours. Remove the meat and vegetables from the Dutch oven and tent with foil. In a cup, mix 2 tablespoons water and cornstarch together until smooth. On the stovetop bring the drippings to a boil. Whisk cornstarch into meat drippings. Stir until desired thickness is reached.

Beef Brisket, Potato Pancakes, Candied Carrots

I like to make this brisket for parties because it is a great "make ahead" meal, since I can make the brisket the day before. I cook the meat, slice it and store it in the gravy. When I am ready to serve, I simply reheat at 350° for half an hour.

Potato pancakes are usually made with flour and eggs, these are not. I have found that keeping some potatoes grated while pureeing the rest works great. I like to make these on a griddle so they are all ready at once. If you don't have a griddle, you can keep the finished pancakes warm in a 200° oven while cooking the rest.

Candied carrots are sweet and tender with a hint of orange flavor. When you are making these, be sure to watch them closely once the liquid has evaporated or they will burn.

Beef brisket
Timing to table: 2 ½ hours
Serves 4

2 lb beef brisket
1 large onion, sliced
1 large carrot, peeled and sliced
4 cloves garlic, whole
2 T tomatoes paste
1 T vegetable oil
2 c beef stock
½ c red wine
2 T water
2 T cornstarch
1 bay leaf
½ t dried thyme
1 t salt
½ t pepper

Preheat the oven to 325°. Season the beef with salt and pepper. In a large Dutch oven high heat, sear the meat on both sides. Remove the meat from the pan and reserve on the side. Lower the heat to medium, and add vegetable oil, onions, carrots and garlic. Sauté 10 minutes until golden. Add red wine to de-glaze the pan. Reduce the wine by half, and add the tomato paste, bay leaf and thyme. Return the beef to pan and add beef stock. Bring the stock to a boil, cover and bake in the oven for about 2 hours or until fork tender. Remove the meat and allow to rest 10 minutes. In a cup, whisk the water and cornstarch together until smooth. On the stovetop, bring the drippings to a boil. Whisk in the cornstarch and water. When the gravy is the desired consistency, slice the meat and return it to the pan, coating with the gravy.

Potato pancakes
Timing to table: 30 minutes
Serves 4

4 medium Yukon Gold potatoes, peeled
½ small onion, quartered
1 T vegetable oil

¼ t garlic powder
½ t salt
¼ t pepper

Grate 2 of the potatoes with a box grater. Dice the other 2 potatoes. Combine the 2 diced potatoes with salt, pepper, onion and garlic powder in the food processor. Process for 1 minute or until smooth. Mix in the grated potatoes. In a large skillet or on a griddle, heat the vegetable oil. Ladle the potatoes in pancake size rounds onto the griddle. Cook over medium heat 10 minutes. With a spatula, turn the potato pancakes and cook an additional 10 minutes.

Candied carrots
Timing to table: 20 minutes
Serves 4

8 medium carrots, peeled and sliced into rounds
1 T margarine
¼ c orange juice
¼ c ginger ale
1 T sugar
½ t salt

In medium sauté pan combine carrots, margarine, orange juice, ginger ale, sugar and salt. Bring to a boil over high heat. Reduce the heat to low, cover and simmer 10 minutes stirring occasionally until the carrots are tender. Remove the lid, increase the heat to medium and allow the liquids to reduce to a glaze, about 5 minutes.

Roast Beef, Scalloped Potatoes, Snow Peas

This is just a basic roast beef. I like my roast beef rare or medium rare. If you prefer yours more cooked, simply increase the cooking time until the desired temperature is reached. Remember that the temperature rises at least another ten degrees while the roast is resting.

These scalloped potatoes are made with beef stock rather that a more traditional cream sauce. The caramelized onions give an added flavor to the potatoes, and the bacon adds even more flavor and prevents the potatoes from drying out on top.

Snow peas are a light and crispy vegetable. They cook quickly and can accompany many different dishes. I like the freshness of these with the richness of the potatoes and beef.

Roast beef

Timing to table: 45 minutes
Serves 4

2 lb eye of round beef roast
2 cloves garlic, sliced
½ t salt
¼ t pepper

Preheat the oven to 425°. Make small incisions in beef roast and insert garlic slices. Season the roast with salt and pepper. In medium roasting pan, roast the beef for 40 minutes or until it reaches an internal temperature of 125° for medium rare. Remove roast from the pan and allow to rest for 10 minutes before carving.

Scallop potatoes

Timing to table: 1 ½ hours
Serves 4

4 medium Yukon Gold potatoes, peeled
4 slices bacon
1 large onion, sliced
1 T margarine
2 c beef stock
½ t dried thyme
¼ t garlic powder
1 t salt
¼ t pepper

In a medium sauté pan over medium heat, heat margarine. Add onions, thyme, ½ teaspoon salt and pepper and sauté the onions until golden brown, about 20 minutes.

Preheat the oven to 425°. Slice potatoes as thinly as possible and season with ½ teaspoon salt and garlic powder. Layer half the potatoes in a casserole dish and spread on all the onions. Top with the remaining potatoes.

Place bacon on a paper towel in the microwave for 2 minutes just to remove some of the bacon fat. Lay the bacon over the potatoes. Pour beef stock over the potatoes and bake for 45 minutes or until potatoes are tender and the bacon is crisp.

Snow peas

Timing to table: 15 minutes
Serves 4

1 lb snow peas
2 scallions, chopped
2 T margarine
2 T water
1 T sugar
½ t salt
¼ t pepper

In a medium skillet, melt margarine over medium-high heat. Add snow peas, scallions, sugar, salt and pepper. Stir to coat the snow peas with the melted margarine. Add the water. Cover and simmer 2 minutes. Remove the cover and boil until the water evaporates, about 2 more minutes.

Pork

Smothered Pork Chops, Herbed Rice, Chopped Salad

Pork chops are one of my family's favorite dinners. These chops are slowly braised so they are extremely tender, and then they are smothered in a mushroom and onion gravy.

I like to pair this with rice to soak up the gravy. I make my rice for this recipe just as I would pasta. I make sure there is enough water to cook the rice, and when the rice is tender I drain it for perfect rice every time. There is no need for precise measuring or a fancy rice cooker. Cooking rice in this manner also reduces the cooking time considerably.

My chopped salad has plenty of vegetable. I like chickpeas in my salad for a meaty taste. The dressing for this salad is a hearty roasted garlic vinaigrette.

Smothered pork chops
Timing to table: 2 hours
Serves 4

4 pork chops, 1 inch thick
2 large onions, sliced
8 oz mushrooms, sliced
2 cloves garlic, minced
1 T vegetable oil
2 c chicken stock
2 T water
2 T cornstarch
½ t salt
¼ t pepper

Season pork chops with salt and pepper. In a large sauté pan over high heat, sear the pork until brown on both sides. Remove the pork from pan and reserve on the side. Lower the heat to medium and add vegetable oil, mushrooms and onions. Cook 15 minutes or until golden. Add garlic and return pork chops to the pan. Add chicken stock, reduce heat to low, cover and simmer 1 hour or until fork tender. Remove chops from the pan. Increase heat to high and bring the drippings to a boil. In a cup, whisk together cornstarch and water until smooth. Whisk into the pan. Stir until desired thickness is reached, then pour over the pork chops.

Herbed rice
Timing to table: 30 minutes
Serves 4

1 c white rice
2 qts water
1 T margarine
1 t salt
1 t dried sage
1 bay leaf
1 t fresh parsley

Bring water to a boil over high heat. Add rice, salt, sage and the bay leaf. Reduce heat to medium and boil for 20 minutes or until the rice is tender. Drain the rice and remove the bay leaf. Stir in margarine and sprinkle parsley over the top.

Chopped salad

Timing to table: 2 hours
Serves 4

1 head romaine lettuce, chopped
1 cucumber, diced
1 carrot, diced
1 tomato, diced
1 bell pepper, diced
2 scallions, sliced
1 c garbanzo beans

Dressing

1 entire bulb of garlic
¼ c + 1 T olive oil
3 T balsamic vinegar
1 T fresh parsley
½ t sugar
½ t salt
¼ t pepper

Preheat the oven to 475°. Cut the bulb of garlic in half crosswise into a top and bottom. Place the garlic halves on a sheet of aluminum foil, and add 1 tablespoon olive oil. Enclose the garlic in the foil. Roast the garlic until golden and soft, about 45 minutes. Allow the garlic to cool slightly. Squeeze the garlic out of the bulb onto a cutting board. With the side of a knife mash the garlic and the salt together. Scrape the garlic and salt into a small bowl. Add vinegar, sugar, pepper and parsley. Whisk in the olive oil.

In a large bowl, combine lettuce, cucumber, carrot, tomato, green pepper and garbanzo beans. Pour dressing over top and toss.

Stuffed Pork Chops, Basmati Rice

My husband loves pork chops, so I am always trying new and different ways to make them. These have a delicious stuffing that doubles as your vegetable. I have made this with frozen spinach, but the fresh spinach cooked in the garlic and oil enhances the flavor. I like to serve this with rice for a complete meal.

For this recipe, I like a basmati rice because the grains remain separate. I add just a little margarine and chives to the rice.

Stuffed pork chops
Timing to table: 45 minutes
Serves 4

4 pork chops, boneless
1 lb fresh spinach, washed
6 mushrooms, diced
2 cloves garlic, minced
1T olive oil
1 c chicken stock
1 T water
½ lemon, zested
1 T lemon juice
1 T cornstarch
2 t Dijon mustard
¼ t dried thyme
½ t salt
½ t pepper

In a medium sauté pan over medium heat, heat olive oil. Add mushrooms and sauté until browned, about 5 minutes. Add garlic and cook until it begins to turn golden, about 1 minute. Add the spinach, salt, pepper, and thyme. Cook until spinach begins to wilt, about 2 more minutes. Transfer the mixture to a medium bowl.

Use a sharp knife to cut a pocket into the pork chop. Stuff each pocket with ¼ of the spinach and mushroom mixture and close the pork chop around the stuffing. In a medium sauté pan over medium high heat, brown the pork chops on both sides. Add stock, mustard and lemon zest to the pan and bring to a boil. Reduce the heat to low, and simmer for 20 minutes or until the pork reaches an internal temperature of 140°. Remove the pork and tent with foil. In a cup, whisk together the water, cornstarch and lemon juice. Whisk into the pan drippings.

Basmati rice
Timing to table: 25 minutes
Serves 4

1 c basmati rice

2 qts water
1 T margarine
1 T chives, chopped
1 t salt
¼ t pepper

Combine the rice, salt and water in a medium saucepan. Bring the water to a boil over high heat; reduce the heat to medium and cook for 15 minutes or until the rice is tender. Drain the rice and add margarine, chives and pepper.

Pork Tenderloin, Baked Beans, Acorn Squash

This pork tenderloin is marinated in a zesty herb rub and then roasted to medium rare. I use coriander in this recipe, which is the seed of the cilantro plant. Because the pork cooks so quickly and is so tender, this recipe is also works great on the grill.

I love baked beans with pork, and these are a true homemade version. The recipe can easily be doubled for large parties. I have had two mother-in-laws in my life, both of whom are wonderful! I have combined their recipes for baked beans here to create one that is really remarkable.

Acorn squash is a sweet winter squash. I like them filled with brown sugar and cinnamon. When checking for doneness, be careful not to pierce the bottom of the squash or all the wonderful sugar will run out.

Pork tenderloin
Timing to table: 3 hours
Serves 4

2 lb pork tenderloin
1 clove garlic, minced
1 T olive oil
1 t coriander
½ t cumin
½ t dried thyme
½ t dried oregano
1 t salt
¼ t pepper

Combine olive oil, garlic, coriander, cumin, oregano, thyme, salt and pepper together. Rub the spice mixture into the pork. Cover the pork and refrigerate. Let marinate at least 2 hours.

Preheat the oven to 425°. Heat an oven safe skillet over medium-high heat. Sear the pork on all sides. Transfer the pork to the oven and roast for 20 minutes or until the internal temperature reaches 140°. Allow to rest for 10 minutes before carving.

Baked beans
Timing to table: 1 hour
Serves 4

1 (14-oz) can navy beans, drained
1 small onion, diced
3 slices bacon
1 T molasses
¼ c ketchup
1 ½ t *Lea and Perrins* Worcestershire sauce
2 T brown sugar
1 t dry mustard
Dash cinnamon
½ t salt
¼ t pepper

Preheat the oven to 425°. Combine molasses, dry mustard, ketchup, Worcestershire sauce, brown sugar, salt and pepper in a medium bowl. Add the beans and onions to the bowl and mix carefully. Transfer the beans to a casserole dish.

Lay the bacon slices on a paper towel in the microwave and cook for 2 minutes. Layer the bacon on top of the beans. Bake 40 minutes or until the bacon is crispy.

Acorn squash
Timing to table: 50 minutes
Serves 4

2 acorn squash, halved and seeded
1 T margarine
½ c water
1 T brown sugar
½ t cinnamon

Preheat the oven to 425°. Place the acorn squash in a casserole dish cut side up. Fill the center of the squash with brown sugar and cinnamon. Top the sugar and cinnamon with the margarine. Pour the water around the squash. Cover the dish with foil and bake for 25 minutes. Remove the foil and bake another 15 minutes or until tender.

Pork Tenderloin and Apples, Sweet Potatoes Oven Fries, Broccoli with Sage

I have always been a fan of pork chops and apple sauce. This is a spin on that, combining the two flavors into one dish. I cook a pork tenderloin with a homemade apple sauce. If you notice the apple sauce getting too thick, add a little water to the pan.

These sweet potato oven fries are crispy on the outside and creamy on the inside. I like to add garlic powder to these to balance out their sweetness.

We have a lot of broccoli in our house. This recipe has some extra flavors that really sets it apart. The sage browns and really flavors the broccoli, so I would highly recommend using only fresh sage in this dish.

Pork tenderloin and apples
Timing to table: 1 hour
Serves 4

2 lb pork tenderloin
2 apples, peeled and diced
½ c chicken stock
1 T lemon juice
1 inch knob ginger, whole
1 T brown sugar
⅛ t cinnamon
Pinch nutmeg
½ t salt
¼ t pepper

In a small sauce pan, combine the apples, lemon juice, ginger, sugar, chicken stock, cinnamon and nutmeg. Bring the sauce to a boil, reduce heat to simmer, cover and cook 30 minutes.

Preheat the oven to 425°. Season the pork with salt and pepper. In large oven safe skillet over high heat, sear meat on all sides. Pour the apple mixture over the pork tenderloin. Transfer the skillet to the oven and roast for 20 minutes, or until the pork reaches an internal temperature of 140°. Allow to rest for 10 minutes before carving.

Sweet potatoes oven fries
Timing to table: 30 minutes
Serves 4

2 large sweet potatoes. cut into wedges
1 T olive oil
¼ t garlic powder
½ t salt
¼ t pepper

Preheat the oven to 425°. Mix sweet potatoes with olive oil, pepper, garlic powder and salt. Spread sweet potatoes on a cookie sheet and roast for 25 minutes turning once or until crispy.

Broccoli with sage
Timing to table: 30 minutes
Serves 4

1 lb broccoli, cut into florets
½ small red onion, sliced`
2 cloves garlic, sliced
2 T olive oil
2 T water
1 T fresh sage leaves, chopped
½ t salt
¼ t pepper

Combine broccoli and water in a covered microwave safe dish. Microwave for 4 minutes or until broccoli is tender. Remove the broccoli from the water and dry on a paper towel.

In a medium sauté pan, heat olive oil over medium heat. Sauté the onions 10 minutes or until golden. Add sage and garlic and cook 5 minutes or until garlic begins to brown. Add broccoli, salt and pepper and sauté for 3 minutes.

Roast Pork & Potatoes, Roasted Beets

This is a lovely sage flavored pork roast. Because the potatoes are cooked with the pork, the pork juices baste the potatoes as they are roasting. I like my pork cooked to medium, so I remove mine at 140° from the oven.

Beets are a root vegetable that are often found pickled in cans. This recipe uses fresh beets only. These roasted beets have a wonderful sweet flavor from the balsamic vinegar. The vinegar helps them finish with a nice brown crust on them.

Roast pork and potatoes
Timing to table: 1 hour
Serves 4

2 lb pork roast
4 medium red potatoes, quartered
1 small onion, sliced
½ t garlic powder
1 t dried sage
1 t salt
½ t pepper

Preheat the oven to 350°. Season the pork with sage, garlic, ½ teaspoon salt and ¼ teaspoon pepper. Place the pork into a roasting pan. Place potatoes around roast and lay the onion on top of the roast. Sprinkle ½ teaspoon salt and ¼ teaspoon pepper over the potatoes. Roast the pork and potatoes about 40 minutes, turning the potatoes once, or until the internal temperature of the pork roast is 140° and the potatoes are tender. Allow the pork to rest 10 minutes before slicing.

Roasted beets
Timing to table: 1 hour
Serves 4

1 lb beets
2 cloves garlic, whole
2 qts water
1 T olive oil
3 T balsamic vinegar
1 t dried rosemary
½ t salt
½ t pepper

Place the beets and garlic into a medium pot and add cold water to cover them. Bring the water to a boil, reduce heat to medium and cook for 20 minutes until the beets are just tender. Drain the beets and discard the garlic. Peel the beets with paper towels and cut them into quarters.

Preheat the oven to 425°. In a medium bowl, whisk the olive oil, rosemary, balsamic vinegar, salt and pepper together to create a dressing. Add the cooked beets to the dressing and mix well. Place the beets on a cookie sheet and bake 30 minutes or until golden.

Sausage and Peppers, Potato Hash, Brussels Sprouts

I typically use an Italian sausage for this dish, although the onions and peppers will work nicely with any smoked sausage. Just be sure to really brown the bell peppers and onions slowly.

I love these crispy potatoes. They mimic the onion and bell pepper flavor of the sausage nicely. I have also served these potatoes in the morning with a breakfast sausage crumbled in for a breakfast hash.

Brussels sprouts are a hearty vegetable that I think taste similar to cabbage. Brussels sprouts also work great with bacon, although what doesn't?

Sausage and peppers

Timing to table: 45 minutes
Serves 4

1 lb sausage
1 ½ green peppers, diced into 1 inch pieces
1 large onion, diced into 1 inch pieces
1 (14-oz) can diced tomatoes, drained
1 t dried basil
½ t dried oregano
½ t salt
¼ t pepper

In a medium sauté pan over medium heat, brown the sausage. Remove the sausage and add the onions and the bell peppers. Sauté the vegetables until golden brown, about 15 minutes. Return the sausage to the pan, and add oregano, basil, tomatoes, salt and pepper. Lower the heat to low, cover, and simmer 20 minutes.

Potatoes hash

Timing to table: 30 minutes
Serves 4

4 medium Yukon Gold potatoes, diced
1 small onion, diced small
½ green bell pepper, diced small
1 clove garlic, minced
2 T vegetable oil
1 t salt
¼ t pepper

In large sauté pan, heat vegetable oil over medium heat. Add potatoes, peppers and onions. When slightly brown (about 10 minutes), add garlic, salt and pepper. Continue cooking an additional 10 minutes, stirring often, until potatoes and tender and browned on all sides.

Brussels sprouts
Timing to table: 25 minutes
Serves 4

1 lb Brussels sprouts, outer leaves removed
3 slices bacon, diced
1 shallot, diced
½ c chicken stock
¼ t salt
¼ t pepper

In a medium skillet over medium-high heat, brown bacon. Remove the bacon and reserve on the side. Add shallots to the skillet and sauté 2 minutes. Add Brussels sprouts, salt and pepper and sauté for 3 minutes. Add chicken stock. Bring the stock to a boil and reduce heat to medium-low. Cook 10 minutes, until tender. Top with the crispy bacon.

Pulled Pork, Carrot Slaw, Baked Apples

This is a Carolina-style pulled pork. The sauce is a delicious and tangy vinegar based sauce, and it goes perfect with the carrot slaw. I have also made this in a slow cooker with excellent results, for those times when I wanted to simply leave it alone all day. With my slow cooker it takes about 6 hours on high or 8 hours on low.

I "have" to eat slaw with my pulled pork, and this meal is designed for both to be eaten together. I really like the carrot slaw, for both the taste contrast and the color. The tangy vinegar sauce of the pork mellows with the sweet carrots. This recipe can be adapted for a cabbage or broccoli slaw if you'd prefer.

Baked apples are a dessert you can eat during dinner. These apples have a cinnamon sugar filling and are then baked until they are soft.

Pulled pork

Timing to table: 24 hours
Serves 8

5 lb pork shoulder
1 c water
1 T brown sugar
2 t white sugar
2 t paprika
1 t garlic powder
½ t ground ginger
½ t onion powder
½ t dried rosemary
½ t salt
½ t pepper

Sauce

¾ c apple cider vinegar
½ c ketchup
¼ c brown sugar
1 T dry mustard
½ t red pepper flakes
1 t salt
½ t pepper

Score the pork fat with a knife. Combine 1 tablespoon brown sugar, white sugar, paprika, garlic powder, ½ teaspoon salt, ½ teaspoon pepper, ginger, onion powder and rosemary. Rub the spice mixture into the pork shoulder. Marinate, covered, overnight in the refrigerator.

Preheat the oven to 425°. Place pork in a roasting pan, skin side down, and roast uncovered for 20 minutes or until lightly browned. Reduce the heat to 325°, turn pork fat side up and add water to the pan. Cover tightly with foil and braise for 3 hours. When extremely tender, remove from the oven and allow to cool slightly. Pull the pork with two forks into shreds. Reserve the pork on the side.

Degrease the meat drippings by lightly skimming the surface with a large spoon. Add vinegar, ¼ cup brown sugar, ketchup, red pepper, mustard, 1 teaspoon salt and ½ teaspoon pepper to the drippings. Bring to a boil, reduce heat to low and simmer 10 minutes. Pour the sauce over the pulled pork

Carrot slaw
Timing to table: 1 ½ hours
Serves 4

8 carrots, peeled
¼ c canola oil
2 T red wine vinegar
1 T Dijon mustard
1 t celery seed
2 T sugar
½ t salt
¼ t pepper

Using a box grater, grate carrots into a large bowl. In small bowl combine mustard, vinegar, sugar, salt, pepper and celery seed. Slowly whisk in the olive oil. Pour dressing over the carrots. Refrigerate for at least 1 hour.

Baked apples
Timing to table: 1 ½ hours
Serves 4

4 apples
4 t margarine
4 T brown sugar
¼ t cinnamon

Preheat the oven to 350°. Core the apples, being careful not to pierce the bottom. Combine sugar and cinnamon. Fill the center of apples with sugar mixture. Place a piece of margarine in each apple. Bake for 1 hour or until tender.

BBQ Ribs, Wild Rice Salad, Roasted Corn

These ribs are given a spice rub, braised in the oven and then bathed in a BBQ sauce. They can be finished on the outdoor grill with excellent results. Once they are tender, transfer the ribs to the grill, baste with the sauce and cook 30 minutes, turning and basting every 10 minutes.

I like a cold salad with my BBQ. This wild rice salad has some wonderful sweet pineapple in it, which creates a wonderful mix of flavors.

I love roasting corn in the oven because it is so easy. I don't have to shuck it before I cook it. After it is cooked the husks come off very easily. The corn works equally well on the outdoor grill.

BBQ ribs and sauce
Timing to table: 24 hours
Serves 4

2 slabs pork spare ribs, 3 pounds each
2 c water
½ c brown sugar
2 T dry mustard
1 t smoked paprika
1 t garlic powder
1 t onion powder
1 t salt
½ t pepper

Sauce

1 c ketchup
⅓ c corn syrup
⅓ c brown sugar
1 t chipotle peppers, minced
¼ c apple cider vinegar
1 T *Lea and Perrins* Worcestershire sauce
1 t smoked paprika
½ t garlic powder
½ t onion powder

Mix together ½ cup brown sugar, dry mustard, 1 teaspoon paprika, 1 teaspoon garlic powder, 1 teaspoon onion powder, salt and pepper in a small bowl. Massage the rub into the ribs and let sit in the refrigerator overnight.

To create the BBQ sauce, combine ketchup, corn syrup, ⅓ cup brown sugar, chipotle peppers, vinegar, Worcestershire, 1 teaspoon paprika, ½ t garlic powder and ½ t onion powder in a small sauce pan. Bring the sauce to a boil, reduce the heat to low and simmer 30 minutes. Refrigerate until needed for the ribs.

Preheat the oven to 350°. Place the ribs on a rack in a large roasting pan. Add water and cover tightly with foil. Cook the ribs, about 2 ½ hours. Uncover and drain any liquid from pan. Increase the heat to 425°. Baste with BBQ sauce and cook ½ hour more basting with BBQ sauce every 10 minutes.

Wild rice salad
Timing to table: 2 hours
Serves 4

1 c wild rice
1 small red onion, finely diced
1 (8-oz) can diced pineapple, drained
3 T vegetable oil
2 qts water
2 T lime juice
1 T brown sugar
2 T fresh cilantro, chopped
1T fresh parsley, chopped
½ t cumin
1 t salt

In a large sauce pan, bring water to a boil over high heat. Add the wild rice; lower the heat to medium and cook uncovered for 35 minutes or until the rice is tender.

Whisk together lime juice, brown sugar, salt, cumin, cilantro, and parsley in a medium bowl. Slowly whisk in the vegetable oil. Add the cooked rice, onion and pineapple. Mix together and refrigerate for at least 1 hour.

Roasted corn
Timing to table: 40 minutes
Serves 4

4 ears of corn in the husk
1 T margarine
½ t salt

Preheat the oven to 425°. Place corn on an oven rack while still in its husks. Roast for 30 minutes. Carefully shuck the corn. Add margarine and salt.

Ham, Potato Salad, Peas

Ham is one of my family's favorite meals. We have it warm for dinner, then cold in sandwiches for the next several days. After that we use the bone to make split pea soup. The ham you buy at the grocery store is already cooked, so we are simply adding some flavor and heating.

This is a warm potato salad which works perfect with the warm ham. The potatoes are cooked and then coated in a warm bacon dressing. Whether or not you peel the potatoes for this potato salad is entirely up to your preference.

Peas are a quick and easy vegetable that are just as good frozen as fresh. I used frozen peas in this recipe. I just thaw before adding them.

Ham

Timing to table: 2 ½ hours
Serves 8

5 lb ham shank
1 c ginger ale
¼ c orange juice
20 whole cloves
½ c brown sugar
1 T Dijon mustard

Preheat the oven to 325°. Place the ham in a large roasting pan and insert the cloves into the ham. Pour ginger ale over the ham. Cover tightly with foil and bake 1 ½ hours. Mix orange juice with mustard and brown sugar. Uncover the ham and spread mustard mixture over the top. Bake 30 minutes until browned.

Potato salad

Timing to table: 45 minutes
Serves 4

4 medium red potatoes
¼ lb bacon, diced
1 small onion, diced
2 cloves garlic, minced
2 qts water
½ c chicken stock
2 T apple cider vinegar
1 T Dijon mustard
1 t sugar
1 t fresh dill, chopped
1 T chives, chopped
½ t salt
¼ t pepper

In a large sauce pan add the potatoes and water. Bring to a boil, over high heat, then reduce heat to medium and cook for 25 minutes until tender. Drain and allow to cool slightly. Carefully remove the skin with a kitchen towel and slice into ½ inch slices.

In a large sauté pan, over medium heat, add bacon and cook until crisp. Remove with a slotted spoon and reserve on the side. Add the onion, salt and pepper to bacon grease and sauté until tender, about 5 minutes. Add garlic and sauté another 2 minutes. Whisk mustard, sugar, chicken stock and vinegar into onions and garlic. Add the potatoes and cook until the dressing is reduced and thickened, about 5 minutes. Add dill, chives and bacon to the pan and carefully mix.

Peas
Timing to table: 15 minutes
Serves 4

1 lb frozen peas, thawed
2 slices bacon, diced
2 shallots, diced small
2 cloves garlic, minced
1 T fresh parsley, chopped
¼ t salt
¼ t pepper

In a medium skillet over medium heat, cook bacon until crispy. Remove the bacon with a slotted spoon and reserve on the side. Add the shallots, garlic, salt, and pepper, and sauté until tender, about 3 minute. Add the peas and sauté until heated through, about 5 minutes. Stir in the bacon and parsley.

Fish

Salmon, Quinoa & Mushrooms, Roasted Parsnips

I was looking for a way to serve salmon that was slightly different. This recipe fit the bill. The marinade for the fish provides a great flavor, and it also allows the fish to brown nicely. The salmon has a sweetness that works great with the savory quinoa.

This quinoa dish is basically a quinoa pilaf. I brown the mushrooms and onions then add the quinoa and broth.

Parsnips are a root vegetable that taste similar to carrots, and roasting them really brings out their flavor. I like to pair the parsnips with mint for added sweetness.

Salmon

Timing to table: 1 hour
Serves 4

4 (6-oz) salmon steaks
2 T olive oil
1 T brown sugar
1 T honey
¼ c Dijon mustard
2 T lemon juice
1 T finely grated ginger
½ t salt
¼ t pepper

Combine the brown sugar, honey, mustard, lemon juice, olive oil, ginger, salt and pepper and whisk until smooth. Coat the salmon on both sides with the sauce and let the salmon marinate for 30 minutes. Heat a large sauté pan over medium heat. Add salmon skin side down and cook 7 minutes. Turn salmon and cook an additional 3 minutes for medium doneness.

Quinoa and mushrooms

Timing to table: 45 minutes
Serves 4

1 c quinoa
1 small onion, diced
4 mushrooms, diced
1 T vegetable oil
2 c vegetable broth
1 t dried thyme
½ t salt
¼ t pepper

Rinse quinoa in cold water. In a sauce pan over medium heat, heat the vegetable oil. Add onions, mushrooms, salt, pepper, and thyme and sauté about 15 minutes or until golden brown. Add quinoa and vegetable broth. Bring to a boil, reduce heat to low and cover. Simmer for 25 minutes.

Roasted parsnips
Timing to table: 30 minutes
Serves 4

1 lb parsnips, peeled and cubed into 1" pieces
1 T olive oil
1 T honey
½ t mint
½ t salt
¼ t pepper

Preheat the oven to 425°. Combine parsnips with olive oil, mint, salt and pepper. Roast for 25 minutes or until tender. Pour honey over the hot parsnips and toss.

Fish and Chips, Roasted Broccoli with Cherry Tomatoes

I love fried food, but the batter usually is a problem for my family. This is a light and fluffy batter for the fish that creates a flavorful crispy crust. I slice the potatoes like potato chips instead of French fries so they are easier to cook. I usually use the same oil for the fish and the chips. I fry the fish first and keep it in a warm oven until the chips are done.

The roasted broccoli is flavored with garlic, salt and pepper. The cherry tomatoes burst while cooking and caramelize, and the two flavors are then mixed together for a really distinctive flavor combination.

Fish

Timing to table: 30 minutes
Serves 4

1 ½ lb firm white fish, cut into 2 inch strips
1 ½ qts vegetable oil
1 ½ c club soda
2 c cornstarch
1 T baking powder
2 t Old Bay Seasoning
1 ½ t salt
½ t cayenne pepper

In a medium bowl, whisk together 1 ½ cups cornstarch and baking powder. Whisk in the club soda until the batter is completely smooth. Refrigerate the batter for 15 minutes.

In a large dish combine ½ cup cornstarch, Old Bay Seasoning, 1 teaspoon salt and cayenne pepper.

In a Dutch oven over high heat, heat vegetable oil to 350°. Lightly dredge fish strips in seasoned cornstarch. Shake off excess cornstarch and dip the fish into the club soda batter. Carefully immerse the fish into the hot oil. When the batter is set, about 2 minutes, turn the pieces of fish over and cook until golden brown, about 4 minutes. Drain the fish on a roasting rack and season with ½ teaspoon of salt.

Chips

Timing to table: 20 minutes
Serves 4

4 large Russet potatoes, very thinly sliced
1 ½ qt vegetable oil
½ t salt

In Dutch oven over high heat, heat vegetable oil until it reaches 320°. Working in small batches, submerge potatoes in hot oil and fry for 3 minutes until they are soft. Remove the potatoes from the oil, drain, and cool to room temperature.

Increase the temperature of the oil to 375°. Re-immerse the fries and cook until crisp and golden brown, another 2 minutes. Remove and drain on a roasting rack. Sprinkle with salt.

Broccoli with cherry tomatoes

Timing to table: 25 minutes
Serves 4

1 lb broccoli, cut into florets
½ pint cherry tomatoes, whole
2 cloves garlic, minced
1 T olive oil
1 T lemon juice
½ t salt
¼ t red pepper flakes

Preheat the oven to 425°. Combine broccoli with cherry tomatoes, garlic, red pepper flakes, salt and olive oil. Spread broccoli and tomatoes on a cookie sheet and roast until the stems are tender and lightly golden brown, about 20 minutes. Squeeze the lemon juice over broccoli.

Marinated Swordfish, Lemon Potatoes, Stuffed Zucchini

Since I can usually only get frozen swordfish from my grocery store, I simply thaw the swordfish in the refrigerator before marinating. Swordfish has a very firm texture, making it ideal for broiling or grilling, and this swordfish recipe works wonderfully on the grill.

These lemon potatoes have a creamy texture and a delicious lemony flavor. The margarine melts over the potatoes and flavors as well as browns them.

Stuffed zucchini is another recipe that I can make early in the day and then simply reheat before dinner. I like to use small or medium zucchini since larger zucchini have more seeds.

Marinated swordfish
Timing to table: 2 ½ hours
Serves 4

4 (6-oz) swordfish steaks
2 cloves garlic, minced
¼ c vegetable oil
2 T lemon juice
1 t dried basil
1 t dried dill
½ t salt
¼ t red pepper flakes

Combine the garlic, vegetable oil, lemon juice, basil, dill, salt and red pepper flakes. Coat the swordfish on both sides and marinate at least 2 hours. Preheat the broiler to high. Broil the swordfish 4 minutes per side.

Lemon potatoes
Timing to table: 35 minutes
Serves 4

4 medium Yukon potatoes, peeled and quartered
2 cloves garlic, minced
2 T margarine, cut into 8 pieces
1 T lemon juice
1 t lemon zest
1 t dried thyme
½ t salt
¼ t pepper

Preheat the oven to 425°. Combine potatoes with lemon zest, thyme, garlic, salt, and pepper. Place potatoes in a casserole dish. Top the casserole evenly with the margarine pieces. Roast potatoes for 30 minutes, turning once. Squeeze lemon juice over the potatoes before serving.

Stuffed zucchini

Timing to table: 30 minutes
Serves 4

2 medium zucchini, halved lengthwise and de-seeded
1 small onion, diced
1 clove garlic, minced
4 oz mushrooms, diced
1 tomato, diced
1 T olive oil
1 t dried basil
¼ t dried thyme
½ t salt
¼ t pepper

In a covered microwavable dish, steam the zucchini in the microwave for 4 minutes or until tender. Carefully scoop out the zucchini flesh, being careful not to tear the skin.

In a sauté pan over medium heat, heat the olive oil. Add onions, mushrooms and garlic and sauté 5 minutes. When softened add the zucchini flesh, tomato, salt, pepper, basil, and thyme. Cook for 10 minutes.

Preheat broiler to high. Fill zucchini halves with tomato mixture and place under the broiler for 2 minutes.

Mahi-Mahi, Eggplant and Jasmine Rice

This is a savory fish stew. The eggplant breaks down and creates a creamy sauce for the fish and rice. The rice and vegetables are fully cooked before the fish is added. This ensures that I don't overcook the fish, and I really nestle the fish down into the rice to surround the fish with heat and flavor.

Mahi-mahi, eggplant and jasmine rice
Timing to table: 50 minutes
Serves 4

4 (6-oz) mahi-mahi filets
1 c jasmine rice
1 eggplant, diced
1 medium onion, diced
1 red bell peppers, diced
1 clove garlic, minced
1 (14-oz) can diced tomatoes
1 T capers
1 T vegetable oil
2 c vegetable broth
1 T fresh basil, chopped
1 T fresh parsley, chopped
½ t dried oregano
½ t salt
½ t pepper

In a large sauté pan, heat vegetable oil over medium heat. Add the onions and bell peppers to the pan. Cook the onions and bell peppers 7 minutes, and then add the garlic. When the garlic begins to brown, add the eggplant and oregano to the pan and continue to cook another 5 minutes. Add the rice, vegetable broth, tomatoes, salt and pepper, to the pan. Bring the broth to a boil, reduce heat to low and simmer for 20 minutes. Remove the cover, raise the heat to medium and stir in the capers, basil and parsley. Add the fish, nestling it into the rice. Cook 10 minutes or until the fish is flaky.

White Fish, Asparagus Risotto

I have made this dish with many different types of white fish, although I prefer a firmer dense fish. It creates a more seared outside and flaky inside, which goes great with the risotto.

Risotto is a dish that is really a lot easier to make than it seems. It does require a lot of attention during the cooking process, but as long as you stir and add the stock slowly, the results will be creamy and flavorful.

White fish
Timing to table: 10 minutes
Serves 4

4 (6-oz) white fish filets
1 T vegetable oil
1 T fresh dill, chopped
½ t salt
¼ t pepper

In a large sauté pan over medium heat, heat vegetable oil. Season the fish with dill, salt and pepper. Add the fish to the sauté pan and cook for 3 minutes per side.

Asparagus risotto
Timing to table: 1 hour
Serves 4

1 ½ c Arborio rice
1 lb asparagus, cut into 1 inch pieces
2 leeks, rinsed well and chopped
1 ½ T olive oil
½ c dry white wine
5 c chicken stock
2 T lemon juice
1 T chives, chopped
½ t salt
¼ t pepper

In a small saucepan over high heat, heat the chicken stock. Bring the stock to a boil and reduce heat to a slight simmer.

In a medium saucepan over medium heat, heat olive oil. Add the leeks and sauté for 10 minutes, or until tender. Add the rice and stir for a minute to coat with the oil. Add the white wine and simmer over low heat, stirring constantly, until most of the wine has been absorbed. Add the chicken stock, ½ cup at a time, stirring often and waiting for the stock to be absorbed before adding more stock. When the risotto has been cooking for 15 minutes, add the asparagus, salt and pepper. Continue cooking and adding stock for another 15 minutes, stirring almost constantly, until the rice is tender and creamy. Stir in the chives and lemon juice.

Tuna Steaks, Mediterranean Quinoa Salad, Roasted Asparagus

Depending on the type of tuna I buy, I vary the cooking times slightly. If I have sushi grade tuna I keep it very rare, cooking about 2 minutes per side. If I have frozen tuna steaks, I cook them about 3 minutes per side.

This Mediterranean quinoa salad is a tangy mix of olives, cucumbers and tomatoes. The soft quinoa compliments the crispy vegetables. The dressing in this salad pairs really well with the tuna.

My kids love roasted asparagus. The tips get crispy while the stems stay tender. Roasting gives the asparagus a slightly nutty flavor.

Tuna steaks
Timing to table: 25 minutes
Serves 4

4 (6-oz) tuna steaks
2 cloves garlic, minced
1 T olive oil
1 lemon, zested
1 T fresh rosemary, chopped
1 T fresh parsley, chopped
1 t salt
¼ t pepper

Preheat the broiler. Combine lemon zest, rosemary, parsley and garlic in a small bowl. Add salt, pepper and olive oil to the herbs. Rub herb and garlic mixture into fish, coating pieces evenly on each side. Broil the tuna steaks 3 minutes on each side

Mediterranean quinoa salad
Timing to table: 1 ½ hours
Serves 4

1 c quinoa
1 c Kalamata olives, pitted and halved
1 cucumber, diced
1 tomato, diced
½ small red onion, diced
2 c vegetable broth
¼ c olive oil
2 T lemon juice
¼ c fresh dill, chopped
2 T fresh parsley, chopped
1 t salt
½ t pepper

Rinse quinoa in cold water. Combine quinoa and vegetable broth in a medium sauce pan over high heat. Bring to a boil, reduce heat to low, cover and simmer 25 minutes or until tender. Transfer quinoa to a medium bowl.

Whisk together the parsley, dill, lemon juice, olive oil, salt and pepper. Pour half of dressing over the still warm quinoa. Refrigerate for 1 hour, or until cool.

Add olives, tomato, onion and cucumber to quinoa and toss with reserved dressing.

Roasted asparagus
Timing to table: 25 minutes
Serves 4

1 lb asparagus
1 T olive oil
¼ t salt
¼ t pepper

Preheat the oven to 425°. Mix asparagus with olive oil, salt and pepper. Spread asparagus in a single layer on a cookie sheet. Roast for 20 minutes, turning often, until tender.

ABOUT THE AUTHOR

Victoria Mazur is a mother of four children ranging in ages from 3 to 25. She was born and raised in the suburbs of Chicago, Illinois, until she tired of the long winters. She currently lives in Wellington, Florida with her youngest children and her husband, Ryan. Victoria can be reached at vmazur13@hotmail.com. Questions and feedback about these recipes are always welcome.

18805818R00107

Made in the USA
San Bernardino, CA
30 January 2015